Fundamentals of Card-not-Present Merchant Acceptance
Edition 2017

Investigation Strategy

Fundamentals of Card-not-Present Merchant Acceptance Edition 2017

Investigation Strategy

Diplom-Kaufmann (FH)
Christian A. Chmiel, CHRU (WSA), CFE, B.A.

&

Markus Prause, CHRU (WSA)

© 2016 Christian A. Chmiel, Markus Prause
Web Shield Services GmbH, Nordstraße 1, D-04105 Leipzig

Editor: Shanty Elena van de Sande, **www.elenavandesande.com**
Co-Editor: Johannes Rosenau

Cover, interior design and print:
Matthias Deuerling, **www.brandcondition.de**

Printed in Germany
ISBN 978-3-9817973-1-2

Executive Summary

As e-Commerce continues to grow at a global scale, so has the volume of CNP payments. E-Shoppers pay merchants for goods and services with an increasing variety of (mobile) devices. Unfortunately, e-Commerce has also proven to be big business for fraudsters who operate in the shadow of the internet boom. Financial regulators continuously update risk protocols, as a wall of defence against fraudulent card holders, deceitful merchants and/or cybercriminals. This has resulted in changing modus operandi of criminals who abuse web shops to test and perfect their fraudulent scenarios; attacks which have had a serious impact on merchant acquirers and payment service providers (PSP) that facilitate merchants' online (CNP) payments.

According to a prognosis based on research by **Nilson Report** for 2015 – 2020: 'In 2020, global card fraud is projected to exceed $35.54 billion. Fraud, grew by 19%, and outpaced volume, which grew by 15%. Fraud losses by banks and merchants on all cards issued worldwide reached $16.31 billion in 2014 when global card volume for the same period totaled $28.844 trillion.'

Payment facilitators hire Risk Managers and Underwriters, in charge of Due Diligence processes and procedures, in compliance with rules and regulations set in place to mitigate risk. Underwriters[1] have become key components in the security protocol of financial institutions.

This 2017 edition of Web Shield's Best Practice Guide for Underwriters aims to support corporate security professionals, who work in risk management teams of financial institutions, such as acquiring banks and payment services providers (PSPs). The previous edition zoomed in on analytical tools and investigative methodology to detect, analyse and prevent fraud. This second edition explores newly discovered Fraud Scenarios. It discusses Transaction Laundering and other forms of malicious Aggregation into great detail. This guide has been written by industry professionals with over a decade of experience in the CNP e-payments sector. While the previous edition explained the fundamentals of a Due Diligence process, this 2017 edition explores additional tools to help analyse and investigate a complex variety of Risk Indicators which have to be validated and assessed during the entire course of an increasingly complex and time-consuming KYC process as part of a company's Customer Identification Program. Underwriters are the first line of defence in the corporate security of the merchant acquiring business. This Best Practices Guide aims to offer a contribution

---

[1] Underwriters, also referred to as Merchant Underwriters, Card-not-Present Underwriters, Merchant Acceptance Manager, Acceptance Manager or Risk Manager.

in protecting financial institutions, card processors, merchant acquirers, and merchants against financial losses and reputational damage. A solid investigation of all risks involved, leads to a well-balanced conclusion to prevent fraud of all types. This ultimately serves to the benefit of all parties involved in e-commerce payments, and last but not least, to protect the card holders.

Contents

Abbreviations..XV

1. Introduction 17
   1.1 Overview...17
   1.2 Preparations..19
2. Investigation Strategy 22
   2.1 Risk Categories 26
   2.2 Risk Indicators..29
   2.3 Primary Risk Indicators..33
        2.3.1   Additional Merchant URLs 33
        2.3.2   Affiliate Networks..34
        2.3.3   Company Formation Agencies...35
        2.3.4   Content Control 37
        2.3.5   Content Violations 38
        2.3.6   Customer Complaints 42
        2.3.7   Deceptive Marketing 46
        2.3.8   Embedded Contact Information 47
        2.3.9   Fake Profiles 48
        2.3.10 Font Cloaking / Font Bumping 50
        2.3.11 Friendly Issuing 52
        2.3.12 Generic Billing Descriptors...56
        2.3.13 Generic Price Points 57
        2.3.14 Mirror Websites...59
        2.3.15 Negative News...61
        2.3.16 Recent Company Formation 62

Contents

		2.3.17	Remittance for Cryptocurrencies	63
		2.3.18	RMA – Return Merchandise Authorization	69
		2.3.19	Sanction or PEP Alert	71
		2.3.20	Shared Contact Details	72
		2.3.21	Stock Images	73
		2.3.22	Social Network Profiles	74
		2.3.23	Subscription Models	76
		2.3.24	Whois Privacy Services	77
		2.3.25	Website Traffic	78
	2.4	Secondary Risk Indicators		80
		2.4.1	Nominee Shareholders	80
		2.4.2	Third Party Billing & Miscoding	82
		2.4.3	Transaction Load Balancing	83
	2.5	Starting the Investigation		92
	2.6	Using the Investigative Risk Analysis		92
		2.6.1	Understand the Business	93
		2.6.2	Collect Data	102
		2.6.3	Research the Data	107
		2.6.4	Analyze the Data and Conclude	117
	2.7	Summarizing the Investigation		123
3.	Online Tools and Sources of Information			128
	3.1	SSL Certificate		128
	3.2	Traffic Source		133
4.	Aggregation			138
	4.1	Compliant Aggregation		138
	4.2	Incompliant Aggregation		139

	4.3	Illegal Aggregation 142
		4.3.1 Transaction Laundering without Miscoding 143
		4.3.2 Transaction Laundering with Miscoding 144
		4.3.3 Third Party Transaction Laundering 146
		4.3.4 Affiliate Transaction Laundering 147
		4.3.5 Competitor Takedown Attack 150
		4.3.6 Merchant Extortion / Blackmailing 153
		4.3.7 Transaction Collection and Testing Attacks 159
		4.3.8 Transaction Weeding Attack 162
	4.4	Aggregation Detection 164
		4.4.1 PULSE Transaction Laundering 164
		4.4.2 Transaction Laundering Incident Alert 165
		4.4.3 Referral URL Screening 166
		4.4.4 Transaction Laundering Investigations 166
5.	Conclusion 169

Glossary 173

About the Authors 179

About the Editors 181

References 182

Recommended Books 185

Recommended Courses 192

Appendix A - Transaction Laundering 194

Appendix B - Flow Chart of the Competitor Takedown Attack 195

Abbreviations

AML	Anti-Money Laundering
BIN	Bank Identification Number
BRAM	Business Risk and Mitigation (MasterCard)
CMM	Chargeback-Monitored Merchant (MasterCard)
CNP	Card Not Present
CTF	Counter-Terrorist Financing
CTR	Chargeback/Transaction Ratio
ECP	Excessive Chargeback Program (MasterCard)
EDD	Enhanced Due Diligence
FAQ	Frequently Asked Questions
FTC	Federal Trade Commission
GBPP	Global Brand Protection Program (Visa)
HTML	Hypertext Markup Language
KYC	Know Your Customer
MATCH	Member Alert to Control High-risk (Merchants)
MCC	Merchant Category Code
PEP	Political Exposed Person
PSP	Payment Service Provider
RMA	Return Merchandise Authorization
SANs	Subject Alternative Names
SSL	Secure Sockets Layer
UBO	Ultimate Beneficial Owner
URL	Uniform Resource Locator
VCMP	Visa Chargeback Monitoring Program
VMAS	Visa Merchant Alert Services
VPN	Virtual Private Network

1. Introduction

1.1 Overview

"Dating operator Lovoo – reported for nearly €1,2M in fraud" was the headline of an article published by German news outlet Heise, on June 6th, 2016[2]. The article outlines the alleged fraudsters' mode of operation: they set up fake profiles in order to incentivize their free users to sign up for a premium account. These allegations solidified and led to two arrests as well as the raid of 16 private homes and corporate offices[3]. The case neatly illustrates the often underestimated financial and reputational risks of merchants who use fake profiles or testimonials. The above example shows how risky negligent underwriting can be.

With this new edition of the "Fundamentals of Card-not-Present Merchant Acceptance" we are introducing a comprehensive investigation strategy, based on the Investigative Risk Analysis (Chmiel, 2010), which highlights what risk indicators an Underwriter should analyze, assess and validate. This new

---

[2] http://www.heise.de/newsticker/meldung/Dating-Dienst-Lovoo-Fast-1-2-Millionen-Euro-Schaden-durch-Betrug-3235838.html (26.08.2016).
[3] http://www.heise.de/newsticker/meldung/Razzia-und-Festnahmen-beim-Dating-Dienst-Lovoo-3231087.html (26.08.2016).

Guide adds online tools and sources to the 16 indicators as outlined in the previous edition.[4] This edition will explore Transaction Laundering or Aggregation into further detail, as fraudsters challenge Risk Managers by inventing new fraud scenarios which have led to complex sophisticated and malicious fraud attacks last year; attacks with a serious impact on both businesses and customers.

As a sequel to last year's "Best Practice Guide for Underwriters", the content of this edition focuses on new developments and advanced investigation techniques. For basic information with regards to investigative methods, we recommend the 2016 edition of the "Fundamentals of Merchant Acceptance". It covers all the basics, such as how merchant acceptance works, details about credit card regulations, how to underwrite merchant applications and other fundamental topics such as document verification, website compliance, financial exposure calculation as well as a multitude of online tools and information sources. It also introduces Transaction Laundering scenarios and ways to detect and analyze Aggregation.

---

[4] Compare section 3.7.1 to 3.7.16 of the Fundamentals of Card-not-Present Merchant Acceptance Edition 2016 (2015).

1.2 Preparations

To mitigate the risk of being tracked by a fraudulent perpetrator, an investigator has to take appropriate precautions; thorough preparation is key to remain anonymous during the course of any online investigation. The risk of being discovered is particularly high, when investigating merchants. Fraudsters can trace data tracks and conceal or alter their online behaviour. To prevent this, the construction of a so-called "virtual second identity" is recommended. In addition to the best practices for preventive measures outlined by Goldman and Borchewski (2008), the following steps are recommended, before starting an investigation.

1. It is recommended to disguise the IP-address of the Underwriter's computer, either with the usage of Proxy Servers, Virtual Private Networks (VPN) or the TOR-Browser[5].
2. The Underwriter should not use services that require log-in or signed-in, particularly on social network sites. The Underwriter should logout and/or delete the associated cookies sites in the web browser.

---

[5] Compare section 3.7.16 of the Fundamentals of Card-not-Present Merchant Acceptance Edition 2016 (2015).

3. Setting up one or multiple fake online identities helps the Underwriter in his work. This includes, but is not limited to fake accounts on social networks to review information about relevant actors and fake email-accounts. Temporary email-account services[6] is another useful tool.[7] The email account is essential for most online sign-up and registration processes, as it has become common practice to send a confirmation email with an activation link which has to be confirmed. It is therefore not possible to successfully activate an account, if the registrant has no access to the provided email-address. Other websites may have implemented more comprehensive anti-fake profile policies, which require SMS verification or similar third steps.

Keeping record of the used fake identities and the gathered user details (such as usernames, passwords, etc.), especially when test transactions[8] are conducted, is highly recommended. A Secure password management tool can be of great help. If a fake profile has already been in place for a few months, future investigations

---

[6] Recommended temporary email services **www.byom.de** and **www.wegwerfemail.de** (24.08.2016).

[7] A fake email-account is recommended though as some temporary email-account services and especially well-known services such as trash-mail.com will often be blocked with the hint that it is not a legit email-address during a sign-up or registration process.

[8] Here, "test transaction" refers to the mystery shopping conducted by the card association in the context of their compliance procedures. By facilitating test purchases on websites that offer illegal goods, the card scheme investigators are able to identify the processing acquiring bank. On the basis of these test transactions, non-compliance actions are taken against any identified acquiring bank.

of a merchant's website can reveal even more relevant information.

2. Investigation Strategy

In some cases, starting an online investigation is the hardest part of the task. In last year's edition, the usage, handling and interpretation of the online research tools and sources below has been described into great detail:

- Whois Information (Section 3.7.1)
- Alexa Scoring (Section 3.7.2)
- Google PageRank (Section 3.7.3)
- Social Bookmarks (Section 3.7.4)
- Social Networks (Section 3.7.5)
- Wayback Machine (Section 3.7.6)
- Reverse-IP Analysis (Section 3.7.7)
- Text Analysis (Section 3.7.8)
- Source Code Analysis (Section 3.7.9)
- Comparing Products with Competitors' Websites (Section 3.7.10)
- Extensive Internet Research (Section 3.7.11)
- Corporate Data Collection Sites (Section 3.7.12)
- Online Complaints Boards (Section 3.7.13)
- Reverse Image Search (Section 3.7.14)

- Google Analytics (Section 3.7.15)
- TOR-Browser and Proxy Server (Section 3.7.16)

Nevertheless, the investigator should be aware of the fact that it's not only important to understand how to use those tools, but also for which purpose and for which type of data.

What risk managers often see, it that the information which an Underwriter is looking for, is hidden from public access. Four reasons have been identified for this phenomenon:

The Right to Be Forgotten

A recent ruling in the EU codified the so called "right to be forgotten".[9] As a result, search engines like Google or Bing have to remove links to specific personal data, in case a person requests it. This data might relate to past criminal activity or other information, negatively affecting an individual's reputation. It is important to note that the information might still be accessible on

---

[9] http://ec.europa.eu/justice/data.../factsheet_data_protection_en.pdf (24.08.2016).

a website, but search engines, the 'gatekeepers' of the internet, will not link to it anymore.

Closed Websites or Missing Indexing

Another reason for this phenomenon is the rise of websites that disallow indexing by search engines (most Facebook content, for example, is not indexed by Google). The same goes for content collected by mobile applications. Nonetheless, many non-indexed services do collect a lot of valuable information, sometimes only accessible to subscribers or customers. Some websites actively try to avoid search engine indexing by either disallowing search engines to index their content (e.g. via the robots.txt file hosted on the root directory of a top level domain), or by avoiding the recording of certain parts of a website (e.g. by embedding the contact details in an image file or by using font cloaking techniques).

Removed Content or Websites

A third reason for this phenomenon is that websites may be offline or some of their content has been removed, after customer complaints or fraud warnings. This can be crucial information for an investigator, as customer feedback is one of the key risk indicators. It is important for an Underwriter to know which online tools are available for historical investigations. An example of such a tool is Waybackmachine[10], which enables the Underwriter to access a past version of an URL

Inhospitable Terms of Service

So called 'Terms of service' (TOS) are another reason for inaccessible data, which legally impedes investigations. The TOS of Facebook is a good example, which states:

> *"If you collect information from users, you will: obtain their consent ..."*

This TOS seems to imply that Underwriters and risk managers are legally obliged to get the researched person's consent before obtaining (public) information from any Facebook page. This obviously obstructs the Underwriter during his/her investigation. Although TOS can be subject to various interpretations,

---

[10] The Waybackmachine can be found on **www.archive.org** (24.08.2016). This Internet archive saves snapshots of the respective URLs at regular intervals, which offers the Underwriter the possibility to access a past version of a URL.

these terms may restrict the collection of information or at least limit its use as evidence in court.

2.1 Risk Categories

Before starting an investigation, it is key to understand **what** the Underwriter is searching for. The current paradigm used by investigators to facilitate merchant Due Diligence procedures as outlined throughout this best practice guide, is often based on **single risk** indicators only. Some of these indicators, such as the number of URLs on an IP address, the visitors on a website or the usage of privacy services stand for themselves and are as such self-explanatory. Nevertheless, missing certain indicators or not seeing their synergies when evaluating a merchant can in some cases lead to a completely different assessment.

Considering the actual origins of merchant underwriting or onboarding, three main risk categories were, and still are, in the focus of an Underwriter:

- Brand Risks
- Chargeback Risks
- Fraud Risks

The above mentioned risk categories also are reflected in several rules and regulations of the card associations, such as the BRAM Program[11] by MasterCard or the GBPP[12] and GMCMP Program[13] by Visa. They therefore have been recognized for years in the area of CNP underwriting.

Nevertheless, we already concluded in last year's "Best Practice Guide" (see Section 5: Financial Exposure Calculation), that a different methodology is necessary to evaluate the holistic risk associated with a given merchant. The associated financial exposure only constitutes a small part of the total risks that a merchant acquirer[14] is facing. In chapter 6 Transaction Laundering is another risk that can have a serious impact on the business of the merchant acquirer. In chapter 3 we described the AML risks, mostly in the context of the identification of the ultimate beneficial owners (UBOs) and the process of screening all associated directors against various sanctions and PEP[15] lists. Working within high risk[16] industries and therefore providing services to

---

[11] BRAM = Business Risk and Mitigation Program (MasterCard).
[12] GBPP = Global Brand Protection Program (Visa).
[13] GMCMP = Global Merchant Chargeback Monitoring Program (Visa).
[14] The "acquirer", "merchant acquirer", "acquiring bank" or "merchant bank" enters into an agreement (merchant agreement) authorizing merchants to accept the association's credit cards, submit their merchants' transactions into the association's interchange system for payment from issuing banks, and maintain accounts and related records on their merchant clients (MasterCard, 2007).
[15] **Politically exposed persons** are understood to be persons entrusted with prominent public functions, their immediate family members or persons known to be close associates of such persons.
[16] According to the Visa Europe Operating Regulations (dated May 15th, 2015) the below MCCs are considered as High Risk Businesses:

high risk merchants as identified in chapter 2, implies reputational risk that needs to be considered. Using different sales channels, selling alternative products and services, specific business risk also needs to be considered when evaluating a merchant. In addition, other risks which do not really fall in one of the identified categories, e.g. a risk due to the lack of PCI DSS compliance, need to be considered.

Following the idea of a holistic merchant investigation, all relevant risk indicators should be identified and considered when evaluating the associated risk of a merchant. Throughout this guide, the below risk categories will be used for classification purposes:

- Business Risks,
- Financial Risks,
- Money Laundering Risks,

5962—Direct Marketing—Travel-Related Arrangement Services;
5966—Direct Marketing—Outbound Telemarketing Merchants;
5967—Direct Marketing—Inbound Telemarketing Merchants (adult entertainment);
7995—Betting, including Lottery Tickets, Casino Gaming Chips, Off-Track Betting and Wagers at Race Tracks;
5912—Drug Stores, Pharmacies;
5122—Drugs, Drug Proprietaries, Druggists' Sundries;
5993—Cigar Stores and Stands, Merchants selling cigarettes in a Card-Absent Environment but excluding such Merchants in Visa Inc. (Canada); and
5993—Cigar Stores and Stands, all Merchants selling cigarettes in a Card-Absent Environment.

- Reputational Risks,
- Transaction Laundering Risks,
- Brand Risks,
- Chargeback Risks,
- Fraud Risks,
- Other Risks.

In the upcoming chapters, the above risk categories will be used to classify the risk indicators which can be collected throughout an investigation.

2.2 Risk Indicators

Investigative risk indicators are classified as primary and secondary indicators. Primary indicators are indicators which do not depend on secondary information to be considered a risk.

> **Primary Risk Indicator Example:**
>
> The identified director of a merchant is queried against a sanction list, which results in a hit. From this, the primary risk indicator "Sanction List Hit" is drawn.

Investigative risk indicators which are classified as secondary (or deductive) are drawn from a combination of two or more primary risk indicators.

> **Secondary Risk Indicator Example:**
>
> The researched address has been identified as the address of an incorporation service or virtual office provider. The primary risk indicator "Incorporation Service Address" is drawn from this fact.
>
> The researched director has also been identified as being active for over 100 additional corporations, registered under the same address. Here the primary risk indicator "Multiple Director Appointments" is drawn.
>
> The research further uncovers the fact that most of the corporations, where the investigated director is engaged are active and operate in completely different business sectors that show no clear relationship to each other. Here, a risk indicator such as "Active in Multiple Business Areas" can be drawn.

> Taking into consideration that,
> - the researched merchant is using an "Incorporation Service Address",

- "Multiple Director Appointments" in various corporations have been identified, and

- these corporations are found to be "Active in Multiple Business Areas" without any clear relationship between them,

- the secondary risk indicator is drawn assuming that the researched director could be considered a "Nominee Director".[17]

The upcoming chapters will provide Underwriters with an overview of the currently most observed and discussed risk indicators in the Card-Not-Present (CNP) merchant acceptance space, up to the date of the publication of this second edition. This book should not be considered as a complete or exhaustive list of all risk indicators, but rather as an overview of current risk trends.

---

[17] A "Nominee Director" is a person that acts as a non-executive director on the board of directors of a corporation, on behalf of another person or another corporation. Additionally, a resident in a tax haven who gives his name to a non-resident as a trustee on the board of an offshore corporation is considered a "Nominee Director". In general, a Declaration of Trust is established between the resident and the non-resident.

At the end of each risk indicator description, a summary is provided that differentiates between primary and secondary risk indicators. Besides providing Underwriters with recommended risk categories it differentiates between risk indicators with a financial, reputational or other impact on the operation of the merchant acquirer. Furthermore, this manual will help you find specific information. Finally, we explain how risk indicators can be removed, amended, controlled, covered, accepted or declined. Risk indicators that cannot be removed, amended, controlled or covered are those that Underwriters refer to when considering the 'risk appetite' of an acquirer.

> **Example:**
>
> The researched merchant has been identified as being registered under the address of a known incorporation service. This fact can neither be removed, amended, controlled nor covered, so either the merchant acquirer accepts the risk of working with a merchant that has been incorporated with an incorporation service or not.

2.3 Primary Risk Indicators

2.3.1 Additional Merchant URLs

In the context of a merchant acquirer's onboarding procedure, the merchant usually has to deliver a full list of processed URLs. This ensures that the acquirer is able to monitor all websites, identify any kind of content violations or illegal services and ultimately prohibit transactions from non-compliant URLs. An acquirer is also submitted to the card association registration procedures, depending on the (High/Low) risk category of the merchant's business.

Identifying additional merchant related URLs that are not known to the merchant acquirer helps to mitigate associated Transaction Laundering risk, as it prevents the possibility that additional and unknown websites will be processed through the merchant account. Depending on the offered service or product and the utilized sales procedure (one-time sales or recurring sales), the anticipated chargeback risk might also decrease.

Risk Indicator:	Additional Merchant URLs
Risk Indicator Classification:	Primary
Risk Category:	Transaction Laundering, Chargeback
Connected Primary Risk Indicators:	none
Impact of the Risk Indicator:	financial, reputational
Mitigation and Proceeding:	control, accept, decline
Common Location(s):	Background research

2.3.2 Affiliate Networks

An affiliate network acts as an intermediary between the advertisers or affiliates and the merchant affiliate programs. It allows website publishers like bloggers or online board operators to participate in revenue generating advertising programs, which are suitable for their website and respective audience. Affiliate networks enable merchants to offer affiliates a share or split of any revenue generated by the merchant from visitors that were funneled through the affiliate's website. Alternatively, they receive a fee for each visitor on the publisher's site that completes a specific action (making a purchase, registering for a newsletter, etc.). Most merchants operate on a revenue share model, as opposed to a fee-per-action model. For merchants, affiliate network services and benefits can include tracking technology, reporting tools, and access to a large pool of affiliates. For affiliates, services and benefits can include simplifying the process of registering for one or more merchant affiliate programs and reporting tools.

Especially in high-risk industries, where user traffic is the most important good, affiliates are generally able to join affiliate networks for free and only have to provide very limited information during the registration process. The fact that the affiliate himself stays nearly anonymous represents a threat and increases the associated Transaction Laundering risk. In addition, high upfront one-time affiliate commissions of 100 to 300 percent of a monthly subscription charge attract fraudulent affiliates that utilize their accounts for affiliate Transaction Laundering attempts.[18] It is therefore important to understand if the affiliate network requires more than just basic information from new members in the sign-up process (such as an email address or a random user name), if they conduct any kind of affiliate Due Diligence and if they monitor the transactions on an affiliate basis in regard of chargebacks, transaction attempts, refunds, etc.

Risk Indicator:	Affiliate networks
Risk Indicator Classification:	Primary
Risk Category:	Transaction laundering
Connected Primary Risk Indicators:	none
Impact of the Risk Indicator:	financial, reputational
Mitigation and Proceeding:	accept, amend, decline
Common Location(s):	Website of the merchant Website of the affiliate network

2.3.3 Company Formation Agencies

Company formation agencies or incorporation services are an easy way to set up businesses or corporations in other jurisdic-

---

[18] Compare section "Affiliate Transaction Laundering Attack" of this guide for more information.

tions. These agencies offer a wide range of services, from the incorporation of the entity to the provision of nominee directors or shareholders. In some cases, they are also offering the sale of shelf corporations. These are aged corporations that were created and left with no activity, until they are sold to the highest bidder. This enables questionable entrepreneurs to start a company, without the necessity to go through all the procedures of creating a new one.

In this context, the widely utilized concept of shell corporations also has an important role to play. Shell companies tend to serve as a vehicle for transactions, without having any significant assets or operations itself. Historically, shell companies have been implemented for tax avoidance purposes, which has become abundantly clear during the Panama Papers revelations[19]. They are also established to maintain a presence in another country or region, without having to relocate the whole business. Some Entities utilize shell companies to gain a merchant account with an acquirer in a foreign country or region to circumvent the Area of Use rules or licensing area of the card associations. As a conclusion, shell companies are part of a range of deceptive

---

[19] https://panamapapers.icij.org/

practices used by fraudsters, criminals and businesses, operating in legal grey areas.

As a result, these should be considered an increased business risk. According to Visa and MasterCard, the utilization of shell companies often creates consumer confusion and can potentially impact interchange and foreign transaction fees.[20]

Risk Indicator:	Company Formation Agencies
Risk Indicator Classification:	Primary
Risk Category:	Business
Connected Primary Risk Indicators:	none
Impact of the Risk Indicator:	none
Mitigation and Proceeding:	accept or decline
Common Location(s):	Search engines (merchant address)

2.3.4 Content Control

Understanding who exactly is in control of the content on a merchant's website is often key to set up appropriate content monitoring tools which allows you to classify the real brand risk that might arise from websites that offer any kind of user generated content. This especially true about websites which offer

---

[20] For more information about the classification of the merchant location please review the MasterCard Revised Standards for Merchant Location, Merchant Disclosure and Area of Use (Global Operations Bulletin, October 1, 2014).

adult entertainment ("Tube Sites") and/or dating services. These merchant types are considered as potential sources of brand damaging content violations (i.e. child abuse) due to uncontrolled user interactions.

If a website offers the upload of user images or videos, it is necessary to clarify if the merchant has any screening procedures in place, to avoid the publication of brand damaging material. The impact of the associated brand risk, depends on the level of content control that is given to the user and the merchant's respective monitoring procedures.

Risk Indicator:	Content control
Risk Indicator Classification:	Primary
Risk Category:	Brand
Connected Primary Risk Indicators:	none
Impact of the Risk Indicator:	financial, reputational
Mitigation and Proceeding:	amend, accept, decline
Common Location(s):	Website terms & conditions

2.3.5 Content Violations

Underwriters refer to 'Content Violations' as a common expression for forbidden or excluded products and services in the context of

a) the MasterCard Business Risk and Mitigation Program (BRAM),

b) the Visa Global Brand Protection Program (GBPP)

c) Applicable underwriting policies (such as the prohibited products and services list of a merchant acquirer).

If a merchant acquirer is caught processing payments for illegal products or services, he risks high penalties and fines in accordance with the rules and regulations of the card associations. Detailed examples for content violations can be found in the MasterCard BRAM program.

The MasterCard Rules[21] state under point 5.11.7.

> *"The Corporation considers any of the following activities to be in violation of this Rule:*
>
> *1. The sale or offer of sale of a product or service other than in full compliance with law then applicable to the Acquirer, Issuer, Merchant, Cardholder, Cards, or the Corporation.*
>
> *2. The sale of a product or service, including an image, which is patently offensive and lacks serious artistic value (such as, by way of example and not limitation, images of nonconsensual*

---

[21] MasterCard Rules – 2015-12-15 - **https://www.mastercard.com/ca/merchant/en/getstarted/BM_Manual.pdf**

sexual behavior, sexual exploitation of a minor, nonconsensual mutilation of a person or body part, and bestiality), or any other material that the Corporation deems unacceptable to sell in connection with a Mark."

Point 1 refers to the fact that every offered product or service needs to be in compliance with the law in the jurisdiction of all involved parties (the Acquirer, the Issuer, Merchant, Cardholder, Cards and the Corporation (MasterCard)). That means that even if the product or service is compliant with the local law in the jurisdiction of the Acquirer, Merchant, Cardholder and Issuer, but not in the jurisdiction of MasterCard, the product or service is in violation of the rules.

Most common examples which may violate this rule are

- Intellectual Property Rights infringements (e.g. cinematic movies distributed via file sharing).
- Sale of counterfeit goods (e.g. counterfeit luxury items, like Rolex or Louis Vuitton.).
- Illegal sale of prescription drugs (e.g. without requesting proof of a valid prescription from the customer).
- Sale of illegal or synthetic drugs or chemicals (e.g. substances listed in Schedule I of the Controlled Substances Act).

- Illegal Internet gambling (e.g. services violating the Unlawful Internet Gambling Enforcement Act of 2006).
- Counterfeit Medical and Dental Devices (e.g. either counterfeit, not approved for sale or expired devices).

Point 2 refers to emotional/pornography content such as videos and images. Images of nonconsensual sexual behavior lead to a wide range of content which might be in violation of the rules, since it is often not possible to determine based on video, image or description alone if consent has been given prior to the displayed actions. Therefore, images or videos displaying individuals under the influence of alcohol or actions with sleeping individuals are often considered in violation of this rule.

Identifying content violations or illegal services can be quite problematic, especially if the merchant is offering a broad variety of products and services on his websites. The application of web crawlers[22] or Merchant Monitoring Service Providers

---

[22] Web Crawlers are automated bots that scan and copy information from websites. They perform web crawling on websites to copy the HTML code, the text and other available content such as images or even videos. An acquirer may use a web crawler to investigate potential content violations on their prospective merchants' websites. Merchant Monitoring Service Providers review and monitor the online merchant's content on their website to identify and address problematic or illegal content that may violate compliance and regulatory requirements. These services are intended for acquiring banks, IPSPs, ISOs and other financial institutions that underwrite merchant applications.

(MMSP)[23] for the detection of BRAM or GBPP violations is recommended.[24] The identification of illegal goods or services, or even circumstantial evidence of their existence (e.g. due to negative historical indicators) increase the overall brand risk and therefore has both a reputational and financial impact on the merchant acquirer.

Risk Indicator:	Website traffic
Risk Indicator Classification:	Primary
Risk Category:	Transaction Laundering
Connected Primary Risk Indicators:	none
Impact of the Risk Indicator:	financial, reputational
Mitigation and Proceeding:	accept, decline
Common Location(s):	Digital marketing services

2.3.6 Customer Complaints

Customer complaints are an important risk indicator since they can give information about many different areas. They can be

---

[23] Principal Members of MasterCard can register Web Shield Limited as an official 'Merchant Monitoring Service Provider' (MMSP) in the Merchant Monitoring Program (MMP). During your participation in the MMP of the BRAM Program, MasterCard may grant some mitigation on assessments for a BRAM and/or Merchant Transaction Laundering violation, provided MasterCard determines that all criteria outlined in the "Merchant Monitoring Program Registration" are met (available to Principal Members only).

[24] For more information about the Web Crawler (SENTINEL, GEiDD, PULSE and Transaction Laundering) and Web Shield please visit **www.webshield.com**.

found on online complaints boards[25], as well as social network profiles. Various factors must be considered:

- The age of the complaint
    - How recent is the complaint or could it be considered outdated?
- The contents of the complaint
    - Does it relate to the current business of the merchant?
    - Is the customer complaining about the product itself, the shipping period or does he not recognize the charge?
- The authenticity of the complaint
    - Has the complaint been copied from somewhere else or could it also be a possible attack by a competitor?
- Additional information arising from the complaint
    - Does the complaint contain additional information relevant to the merchant profile, e.g. previous billing descriptors[26], contact details or websites?

---

[25] Compare section 3.7.13 of the Fundamentals of Card-not-Present Merchant Acceptance Edition 2016 (2015).

[26] The billing descriptor (or merchant descriptor) is the way a merchant's name appears on a credit card statement and is set up together with the merchant identification number when the merchant account is created. It is used by the credit card holder, to identify the merchant that initiated the

The age, the content and the authenticity of the complaint all have an impact on how important the retrieved information is for the Underwriter. Of course, the total number of identified complaints need to be taken into consideration. Obviously, it makes a great difference whether only one, or hundreds of customer complaints are detected. It is recommended to read this number in relation with the total number of visitors[27] of a website:

> During the Due Diligence procedure, the Underwriter discovered seven complaints on **www.ripoffreport.com**. Two complaints related to unauthorized charges and four complaints to delivery delays. By calculating the Alexa scoring, an average daily visitor traffic of 10.000 to 15.000 visitors is detected.

It is crucial to put the total number of website visitors in relation with the total number of identified complaints. This enables the Underwriter to make a decision on how to substantiate and validate the identified complaints.

---

charge. Credit card organizations use the billing descriptor within their monitoring systems (e. g. chargeback or fraud monitoring).

[27] This information can be retrieved by using the Alexa scoring.

In addition to customer complaints that relate to the merchant only (e.g. as they relate to the merchant name, address, phone number, billing descriptor or website), complaints that relate to potentially connected merchants or URLs (e.g. URLs on the same IP address, merchants registered under the same address, merchants sharing contact details such as the phone number, merchants operating mirror websites, etc.) form another risk indicator. These kind of complaints are especially interesting, when the researched merchant incorporated recently or a website has just recently been launched. In this cases, there is usually only a very limited amount of information available. Related entities or websites can give an indication of possible outcomes (especially if they are offering the same product, with the same price points and the same subscription terms, etc.).

Finally, one may not forget that a total absence of complaints can also be a significant risk indicator that needs to be considered, especially when a processing history has been provided.

Customer complaints in general increase the associated chargeback risk, in particular if they are recent and relate to unrecognized or unauthorized charges.

| Risk Indicator: | Customer Complaints |

Risk Indicator Classification:	Primary
Risk Category:	Chargeback
Connected Primary Risk Indicators:	none
Impact of the Risk Indicator:	financial,
Mitigation and Proceeding:	accept, decline, cover
Common Location(s):	Social networks Online complaints boards

2.3.7 Deceptive Marketing

Deceptive or false marketing is the use of misleading, false or deceptive statements when advertising services or products. The most common types of deceptive marketing techniques are

a) Misleading illustrations,

b) Undisclosed or hidden fees (e. g. additional memberships),

c) 'Risk free' or 'no risk' advertisement,[28]

d) High-pressure sales (e.g. timer on a website), and

e) Auto-opt in or acceptance by default (e.g. cross-sales on the payment page).

---

[28] https://www.ftc.gov/news-events/press-releases/2015/06/ftcs-request-court-temporarily-stops-online-skincare-marketers (02.08.2016).

Apart from the obvious reputational risk a merchant acquirer is facing when processing a merchant that utilizes deceptive marketing techniques, it also increases the business and chargeback risks, as for example in cases of auto-opt in or hidden fees, card holders are not aware of any additional charges. They usually only notice the false promises when the product has been delivered, often resulting in immediate chargeback requests.[29]

Risk Indicator:	Deceptive or false marketing
Risk Indicator Classification:	Primary
Risk Category:	Business, Chargeback
Connected Primary Risk Indicators:	none
Impact of the Risk Indicator:	financial, reputational
Mitigation and Proceeding:	amend, remove
Common Location(s):	Website terms & conditions Website payment page Website landing page

2.3.8 Embedded Contact Information

Placing and embedding the merchant details, such as the merchant name, address, contact details, or billing descriptor information, in an image instead of using regular text on a website prevents search engines and online libraries from indexing and matching a website to its respective operator and associated

---

[29] More information about deceptive marketing techniques can be found on https://www.ftc.gov/news-events/media-resources/truth-advertising (02.08.2016).

contact details. It also prevents users, as well as Underwriters, from being able to find a company's name, address or contact details by using a search engine query.

This kind of behavior has been identified as an indicator for transaction load balancing. It enables the fraudster to exchange the corporate information on several sites at once. The practice has been observed in merchants, operating in the areas of health & beauty, adult content, dating, remote PC services and penny auctions. Associated merchants should be considered as having an increased chargeback risk.

Risk Indicator:	Embedded contact information
Risk Indicator Classification:	Primary
Risk Category:	Chargeback
Connected Primary Risk Indicators:	none
Impact of the Risk Indicator:	financial, reputational
Mitigation and Proceeding:	amend, remove, accept, decline
Common Location(s):	Website terms & conditions Website payment page Website contact page

2.3.9 Fake Profiles

As hinted at in the introduction, the usage of fake profiles, even at legitimate seeming dating sites seems to be on the rise. The relative anonymity of online dating, attracts fraudsters who in search of an easy way to make money on the backs of lonely people. In recent cases, we have seen how fake profiles have been generated, connected with chat bots that automatically get in touch with (mostly male) members and eventually encourage them to sign up for a subscription or credit purchase as a condition to be able to interact (e.g. sending emails or messages, unveiling videos or images, etc.) with their false sweetheart.

The risks associated with fake profiles, especially when the merchant does not disclaim it in his terms and conditions, are often either underestimated. The Lovoo case clearly proves that merchants – and their acquiring banks – risk high losses. Losses, which increase explosively when membership programs are involved and users have been utilizing the service for several months.

Risk Indicator:	Fake Profiles
Risk Indicator Classification:	Primary
Risk Category:	Chargeback
Connected Primary Risk Indicators:	none
Impact of the Risk Indicator:	financial, reputational
Mitigation and Proceeding:	amend, remove, accept, decline
Common Location(s):	Merchant website Reverse image research

2.3.10 Font Cloaking / Font Bumping

Font Cloaking or Font Bumping is a technique which aims at preventing search engines or online libraries from indexing and matching the websites to their respective operators. It also prevents users from being able to search for bumped information. Random letters and digits are implemented invisibly (font size 0), which results in a different display text when a search engine or online library bot tries to index the website compared to a normal visitor viewing the website. Font Bumping has the same effect as putting and embedding information in image files.

How can Font Bumping be identified? An easy way is to copy and paste the text in question into a text processing program (e.g. Editor), inspecting the element via a web browser console or with the help of a cloaking checker[30].

---

[30] http://www.webconfs.com/cloaking-checker.php

Example:

The visible company information on the footer of the website sample.com is

"BILLINGYOU LTD, 1119 Sample Drive, Sampleville, UK".

A search engine bot will read the information as

"BI5B6/LL:XCQ   INROENTGYXRO1KVB   OU7ULLLT1MLL, DTE1113CQ19 Sa4mp1pleusBY4 D8VQriBUOve,NYH SaF9or-plPgaeKKMnvil7D0le,VGF UK6HO07"

The random letters and digits are inserted with font size 0, therefore the search engine will not be able to index the merchant name "Billingyou Ltd" but would only show the result if the user was looking for "BI5B6/LL:XCQ".

The usage of font cloaking or font bumping increases the Transaction Laundering risk as it is considered an attempt to disguise the transaction source.

Risk Indicator:	Font Cloaking / Font Bumping
Risk Indicator Classification:	Primary
Risk Category:	Transaction Laundering
Connected Primary Risk Indicators:	none
Impact of the Risk Indicator:	financial, reputational
Mitigation and Proceeding:	amend, remove
Common Location(s):	Website terms & conditions Website payment page Website landing page

2.3.11 Friendly Issuing

Another performance optimization tactic where certain monitoring procedures of the merchant acquirer or the card associations are circumvented is Friendly Issuing. This method is used to stay out of certain Card Scheme programs such as Visa's Visa Chargeback Monitoring Program (VCMP) and MasterCard's Excessive Chargeback Program (ECP). Both programs are calculated based on the chargeback-to-transaction ratio (CTR) of a merchant. Their aim is to identify merchants with excessive chargeback's.

Friendly Issuing exploits the calculation method by increasing the transaction count, in order to reduce the whole ratio. Usually prepaid cards are issued and loaded. In the next step, transactions with small ticket sizes are processed on the merchant account, which exceeds the threshold of a Card Scheme program. The upcoming examples are based on the MasterCard Excessive Chargeback Program (ECP) calculation. In this case, the chargeback-to-transaction ratio is calculated based on the number of MasterCard chargebacks received by the acquirer for a merchant in a calendar month, divided by the number of the merchant's MasterCard sales transactions in the preceding month.[31]

Example without Friendly Issuing:

Preceding month's transaction count: 15.000

Current month's chargeback count: 200

The merchant ABC Limited operates dating services. In the preceding month he has processed 15.000 MasterCard transactions. In the current month, 200 chargebacks have been reported. The chargeback-to-transaction ratio would be at 1,33 percent. As the merchant exceeds the 100 basis points and 100 chargebacks in a calendar month he is considered a Chargeback-Monitored Merchant (CMM) under the Excessive Chargeback Program.

---

[31] MasterCard Security Rules and Procedures - Merchant Edition – 2016-03-31

> **Example with Friendly Issuing:**
>
> Preceding month's transaction count: 15.000
>
> Friendly issued transactions: 10.000
>
> Total transaction count: 25.000
>
> Current month's chargeback count: 200
>
> The merchant ABC Limited operates dating services. In the preceding month he has processed 15.000 MasterCard transactions. In addition to that, he has also processed 10.000 additional 1,00 USD transactions on his own issued cards.
>
> In the current month, 200 chargebacks have been reported. The chargeback-to-transaction ratio would be at 0,80 %. As the merchant does not exceed the 100 basis points he is not placed under the Excessive Chargeback Program.

Due to the fact that MasterCard calculates the basis points based on the transaction count of the preceding month, it is more difficult to calculate the amount of transactions which are required to not exceed the threshold.

The Visa Chargeback Monitoring Program (VCMP) is calculated based on transaction and chargeback count within the same month, thus it is easier to avoid the program, as the required number of transactions can be calculated precisely at the end of each month.

However, friendly issuing often attracts the attention of the Card Schemes as they notice Bank Identification Number (BIN) concentrations, if the cards used for Friendly Issuing have the same or only a limited number of different BINs. Additionally, the date of the transactions can be a strong indicator, because it is easier to forecast how many transactions are required to avoid the enrollment into a chargeback monitoring program. The transactions in question, are usually placed at the end of a calendar month.

Friendly Issuing increases the merchant acquirer's reputational and financial risk. The acquirer could be held liable for penalties from card associations, because of the violation of monitoring programs. Indications for Friendly Issuing attempts can be drawn from historical processing statements, in which a high number of low amount transactions have all been processed in the last days of each month. These can also be detected by putting an appropriate transaction monitoring procedure in place.

Risk Indicator:	Friendly Issuing
Risk Indicator Classification:	Primary
Risk Category:	Business, Transaction Laundering
Connected Primary Risk Indicators:	None
Impact of the Risk Indicator:	financial, reputational
Mitigation and Proceeding:	control
Common Location(s):	Processing History Transaction Monitoring

2.3.12 Generic Billing Descriptors

A billing descriptor is considered as generic, when the merchant or the website cannot be uniquely identified by the card holder. In addition to that, the usage of generic billing descriptors sidesteps the identification of customer feedback or complaints for the Underwriter.

> **Example:**
>
> The merchant Sample Limited is requesting the billing descriptor 'Great Product'. This would be considered generic, as it is not possible to clearly identify the merchant, the website nor the product that has been purchased. Researching the term 'Great Product' will to identify the associated website or merchant will with a high probability not yield usable results.

This also impedes the search for customer feedback or complaints, as the number of search results would be too big to simply sift through.

Generic billing descriptors increase the chargeback risk, as the card holder might not recall the charge and is therefore more likely to initiate a chargeback. Often, the card holder doesn't know how to get in touch with the merchant for further clarification or refund purposes.

Risk Indicator:	Generic billing descriptor
Risk Indicator Classification:	Primary
Risk Category:	Chargeback
Connected Primary Risk Indicators:	none
Impact of the Risk Indicator:	financial
Mitigation and Proceeding:	amend, decline
Common Location(s):	Website payment page Merchant acceptance contract

2.3.13 Generic Price Points

Generic price points are round totals for the products and services a merchant is offering (e.g. 25 EUR, 50 EUR, 100 EUR, etc.).

> **Example:**
>
> The merchant IT Geek Limited claims to offer Remote PC Services. The price points for the services on the website are
>
> 25 USD one-time fee for 1 Computer
>
> 50 USD for 3 Computer
>
> 75 USD for 6 Computer
>
> 100 USD for 10 Computer
>
> These price points can be considered generic, as they could also match the transactions of a gambling operator.

Generic price points per se are not considered a serious issue, but in combination with other factors such as generic billing descriptors or identified mirror websites, it is a possible indication for miscoding behavior and therefore increases the Transaction Laundering risk.

Risk Indicator:	Generic price points
Risk Indicator Classification:	Primary
Risk Category:	Transaction laundering
Connected Primary Risk Indicators:	none
Impact of the Risk Indicator:	financial, reputational
Mitigation and Proceeding:	Control
Common Location(s):	Website product section or overview

2.3.14 Mirror Websites

According to webopedia.com, a mirror website is a website that is a replica of an already existing site under a different URL, used to "reduce network traffic (hits on a server) or improve the availability of the original site. Mirror sites are useful when the original site generates too much traffic for a single server to support."[32]

Example:

If www.abc.com and www.123.com each have the identical content, but are on different servers, they are considered mirror sites.

---

[32] http://www.webopedia.com/TERM/M/mirror_site.html (03.08.2016).

Underwriters pay extra attention to mirror websites, when they are in fact a replica or copy of an existing site, but with a merchant selling goods and/or services under a different name, address, etc.

> **Example:**
>
> www.abc.com and www.123.com each have the identical content, offer the same products with the same price points and are hosted on different servers. The website www.abc.com displays the merchant name "ABC Limited" with an address in the United States whereas www.123.com displays the merchant name "One Two Three Limited" with contact details in the United Kingdom.

In most cases, such mirror websites aren't set up for the purpose of reducing network traffic, but to gain multiple acquirer relationships for transaction load balancing[33] or Transaction Laundering purposes.

In addition, mirror websites have also been observed of being used as credit card data collection or phishing sites, where

---

[33] Please refer to the chapter "Transaction Load Balancing" for more information.

known brand websites are copied and made accessible online for a short time, just for the purpose of collecting card holder data for fraudulent purposes.

The assessment of mirror websites makes it necessary to understand the purpose of these websites to be able to evaluate the associated risk. The presence of a mirror website with different merchant details is considered by Underwriters as a primary risk indicator for chargeback as well as for Transaction Laundering risk.

Risk Indicator:	Mirror Websites
Risk Indicator Classification:	Primary
Risk Category:	Business, Chargeback, Transaction Laundering
Connected Primary Risk Indicators:	none
Impact of the Risk Indicator:	financial, reputational
Mitigation and Proceeding:	accept or decline
Common Location(s):	Search engine research Plagiarism research (copyscape.com)

2.3.15 Negative News

Negative news, scam or fraud warnings, as well as information on criminal charges relating to the merchant, the directors or beneficial owners, are useful sources for additional relevant merchant-related information. In this context, it is important to verify how reliable the source of the negative news is. Are these sources trustworthy? How old are these reports and could they be linked to an aggressive competitor? The Underwriter should verify the authenticity of negative claims during the course of his investigation. In any case, negative reports tend to increase both chargeback- and business risk and have to be considered as primary risk indicators.

Risk Indicator:	Negative news
Risk Indicator Classification:	Primary
Risk Category:	Business, Chargeback
Connected Primary Risk Indicators:	none
Impact of the Risk Indicator:	reputational
Mitigation and Proceeding:	accept, decline
Common Location(s):	Background research Adverse media lists

2.3.16 Recent Company Formation

In the context of this Guide, a company is considered 'recently formed' if the incorporation (certification) has taken place less than 12 months ago. Risk, associated with a recently formed entity is mainly financial. In general, there is no historical data about business practices or the processing of the company available, which complicates the calculation of the required collaterals. As a consequence, some acquirers refrain from offering merchant accounts to startups or to recently incorporated companies.

Risk Indicator:	Recent Company Formation
Risk Indicator Classification:	Primary
Risk Category:	Business, Finance
Connected Primary Risk Indicators:	none
Impact of the Risk Indicator:	financial
Mitigation and Proceeding:	accept or decline
Common Location(s):	Incorporation Documents

2.3.17 Remittance for Cryptocurrencies

A cryptocurrency is a medium of exchange, which uses cryptography to secure transactions (Blockchain) and control the creation of new crypto units (mining). Cryptocurrencies are a subset of virtual currencies, e.g. World of Warcraft gold or similar digital tokens. Historically, the first decentralized cryptocurrency was Bitcoin, which was introduced by Satoshi Nakaomoto, back in 2009[34]. Since then, numerous cryptocurrencies have been cre-

---

[34] You can find the original white paper "Bitcoin: A Peer-to-Peer Electronic Cash System" here: https://bitcoin.org/bitcoin.pdf

ated. In an allusion to their predecessor, they are commonly referred to as 'altcoins'.[35] Cryptocurrencies are generally organized in an open peer-to-peer system, as opposed to centralized banking.

As cryptocurrencies are becoming mainstream, financial authorities and regulators are forced to pass new legislation to protect consumers and local businesses around the globe. As a result, the legal status of cryptocurrencies varies substantially from country to country and is still undefined or subject to discussion in many jurisdictions. While some countries have explicitly allowed their use and trade, others have banned or restricted it. Government agencies, departments and courts classify the risk posed by cryptocurrencies differently. In the US, Bitcoin is regarded as property. As such, it isn't subject to the same taxation as currency. –Even though cryptocurrencies are legal in Russia, it is illegal to purchase goods with any currency other than the Russian ruble. The government's legal view on cryptocurrencies is constantly shifting between begrudging tolerance and calls for a total ban[36]. In general, cryptocurrency networks are still in the process of being subjected to financial rules

---

[35] A full list of current cryptocurrencies available on https://en.wikipedia.org/wiki/List_of_cryptocurrencies.
[36] A helpful resource concerning the legal status of Bitcoin around the world is http://map.bitlegal.io/.

and new regulations. This is why such networks attract individuals and entities in search of privacy-friendly, decentralized currency. Critics regard cryptocurrencies as tools which facilitate tax evasion and money laundering.

One of the main reasons for such allegations is the quasi-anonymity[37] which cryptocurrencies offer their users. For criminals, using Bitcoin to launder money can seem like an attractive alternative, as it saves them from having to construct an intricate net of financial actors and offshore bank accounts. In order to increase anonymity, 'mixers' and 'tumblers' provide laundering services. They obscure the relationship between input and output addresses, by blending multiple bitcoin sources together.

In the US, there haven't been many cryptocurrency-related arrests yet, mainly because the difficulty of connecting cryptocurrency accounts with their respective account holders. The arrests that have been made are all on charges of using

---

[37] Technically, Bitcoin is a pseudonymous payment method, as all transactions, including the input and output address as well as the amount, are publicly available in the Blockchain. Nonetheless an attacker has to tie the arbitrary addresses to a concrete person, which most of the time is no easy task. Other altcoins like monera afford even more robust anonymity.

cryptocurrency to launder money (see for example the arrest of Charlie Shrem, CEO of BitInstant[38]).

Cryptocurrencies are also a popular exchange medium in 'Dark Net Markets', where they are mainly used to purchase illegal drugs. This fact represents a serious challenge for the reputation of cryptocurrencies and of businesses associated with cryptocurrencies. It is important to emphasize that most of the big bitcoin wallets instantly shut down the accounts of users, suspected of 'Dark Net Market' activity.

On 12 December 2013, the European Banking Authority (EBA) issued a warning, identifying a series of potential risks arising from purchasing, holding or trading virtual currencies. Cryptocurrencies can most easily be acquired directly from a person who already owns them or through an exchange platform. In most cases, this process is not (yet) regulated.

Underwriters should be aware of the following risks, when accepting Legal Entities that are purchasing, holding or trading virtual currencies:

---

[38] https://www.theguardian.com/technology/2014/dec/22/bitcoin-entrepreneur-sentenced-jail (26.08.2016).

Theft and loss of money (increased Chargeback and Reputation Risk): Unlike banks, the cryptocurrency exchange platforms do not hold their virtual currencies as a deposit. As a consequence, in case of money loss from an exchange platform, technical issues or digital theft, the user isn't guaranteed the same legal protection as offered by traditional deposit guarantee schemes, which cover losses of funds processed on trading platforms. A notorious case was Mt. Gox, which had to suspend its operations in February 2014 and left many people without their money.[39] More recently, the Bitcoin exchange platform Bitfinex reported a theft of over $60 Million – a loss they decided to spread evenly amongst all their customers.[40]

Chargebacks / Errors / Unauthorized payments (increased Chargeback and Reputation Risk): In the absence of EU legislation which provides a right to reimbursement, unauthorized or erroneous transactions made from digital wallets cannot be cancelled.

Volatile Exchange Rates (increased Chargeback and Reputation Risk): In general, the exchange rates of virtual currencies

---

[39] http://www.coindesk.com/mt-gox-the-history-of-a-failed-bitcoin-exchange/ (26.08.2016).
[40] http://www.coindesk.com/bitfinex-examined-bitcoin-exchange/ (26.08.2016).

are very volatile, rendering the value of virtual currencies unstable and a risky asset for investors.

Lacking Transparency and offering Relative Anonymity (increased AML Risk): There is only limited traceability for virtual currency transactions, which offers users of virtual currency a high level of anonymity. This makes cryptocurrency attractive for transactions with criminal purposes, such as money laundering.

Limited Compliance Rules and Regulations: Virtual currencies such as bitcoin do not fall within the scope of the EU Electronic Money Directive (2009/110/EC). In a warning to consumers on virtual currencies published on December 12 2013, the EBA defined a 'virtual currency' as: 'a form of unregulated digital money that is not issued or guaranteed by a central bank and that can act as means of payment. Virtual currencies have come in many forms, beginning as currencies within online computer gaming environments and social networks, and developing into means of payment accepted 'offline' or in 'real life'. It is now increasingly possible to use virtual currencies as a means to pay for goods and services with retailers, restaurants and entertainment venues. These transactions often do not incur any fees or charges, and do not involve a bank.' In a February 14 2014 press release, the Luxembourg financial sector regulator (CSSF) stated that 'virtual currencies are considered as money, since they are accepted as a means of payment of goods and services by a sufficiently large group of people'.

Merchants that are providing remittance services for cryptocurrencies therefore pose a higher chargeback, reputation and money-laundering risk for the merchant acquirer. Appropriate controls and identification procedures should be implemented, in order to minimize money-laundering risk (AML) caused by the anonymity of the payment method itself.

Risk Indicator:	Remittance for Cryptocurrencies
Risk Indicator Classification:	Primary
Risk Category:	Chargeback, Reputation, AML
Connected Primary Risk Indicators:	none
Impact of the Risk Indicator:	financial, reputational
Mitigation and Proceeding:	accept, decline, control
Common Location(s):	Website terms & conditions Website payment page Website landing page

2.3.18 RMA – Return Merchandise Authorization

A return merchandise authorization number (RMA) is part of the process of returning a product in order to receive a refund, a replacement or a repair during the product's warranty period. In these cases, the cardholder must contact either the merchant, the fulfillment center, or the manufacturer to obtain the authorization to return the product. The associated RMA number must be displayed on or included in the returned product's packaging as no returns are accepted without it.

The usage of RMA numbers has become a regular occurrence, when underwriting subscription merchants engaged in the sale of nutraceutical (or health & beauty) products. In these cases, the RMA process is used to increase the hurdle of requesting a refund, especially when the merchant is targeting cardholders in jurisdictions where initiating a chargeback is more difficult than in the United States.[41] Using the Return Merchandise Authorization in jurisdictions where it is easy to initiate chargebacks, increases the chargeback risk as an unsatisfied customer will probably simply request a chargeback online instead of going through the whole return procedure.

---

[41] In Germany for example, issuing banks often request their cardholders to provide a police report before they are able to initiate a chargeback.

Risk Indicator:	RMA Numbers
Risk Indicator Classification:	Primary
Risk Category:	Chargeback
Connected Primary Risk Indicators:	none
Impact of the Risk Indicator:	financial
Mitigation and Proceeding:	amend, remove
Common Location(s):	Website terms & conditions

2.3.19 Sanction or PEP Alert

Pursuant to the rules of the card associations, all of their licensed customers, regardless of location, must comply with OFAC regulations as well as local sanctions regimes. They need to screen their merchants, associated directors and beneficial owners (UBO), against the OFAC sanctions lists and any other applicable lists at onboarding and on an ongoing basis as the principal members of the card associations are not allowed to conduct business in sanctioned geographies and to board merchants that have been designated by OFAC.[42]

Any kind of hit on a sanction list, as well as PEP hits need to be investigated into great detail in order to ensure compliance with the card associations' rules. A verified hit on a sanction or PEP

---

[42] For more information, please review Rule 1.2 of the MasterCard Anti-Money Laundering Program.

list is categorized as an increased money-laundering risk (AML).

Risk Indicator:	Sanction or PEP Alert
Risk Indicator Classification:	Primary
Risk Category:	AML
Connected Primary Risk Indicators:	none
Impact of the Risk Indicator:	reputational
Mitigation and Proceeding:	accept, decline
Common Location(s):	Merchant documents ID cards Ownership structure

2.3.20 Shared Contact Details

Shared contact details are considered a primary risk indicator. It refers to contact details uniquely associated with a merchant. This refers to

    a) Phone numbers

    b) Fax numbers

    c) Email addresses

    d) Skype names

Shared contact information can be an indication for third party billing or miscoding. It is therefore important to understand what other businesses or merchants are connected with the contact details. Shared contact details are increasing the associated Transaction Laundering risk.

Risk Indicator:	Deceptive or false marketing
Risk Indicator Classification:	Primary
Risk Category:	Transaction laundering
Connected Primary Risk Indicators:	none
Impact of the Risk Indicator:	financial, reputational
Mitigation and Proceeding:	accept, decline
Common Location(s):	Website contact page Merchant documents Website payment page Background research

2.3.21 Stock Images

Stock images are images that are created and licensed for specific use. Stock agencies charge between a few cents up to several thousand euros per image. Stock images in general are not considered as a risk indicator, as they are used in the promotional materials of many reputable corporations. Their use becomes a meaningful risk indicator, if specific images are replaced with stock images. This applies especially to images claiming to show the registered office of the merchant as well as directors or key personnel.[43] Stock images which are either being used as an image of the registered office address or of that of the directors or employees, increase the associated business and Transaction Laundering risk, as this practice has been observed to be part of third party billing or miscoding schemes.

Risk Indicator:	Stock images
Risk Indicator Classification:	Primary
Risk Category:	Business, Transaction laundering
Connected Primary Risk Indicators:	none
Impact of the Risk Indicator:	financial, reputational
Mitigation and Proceeding:	accept, decline
Common Location(s):	Website contact and about us page

2.3.22 Social Network Profiles

Social network sites are web-based services that allow individuals to create a public or semi-public profile within a fixed system, whereby the nature of the connections between user profiles varies from site to site (Haythornthwaite, 2005). Facebook, Twitter, LinkedIn, Xing and Google+ are among the biggest and

---

[43] Reverse image search engines like Google Image Search or TinEye search the web for the same or similar images. Image files can either be uploaded directly to the search engine or the URL-link of the image can be inserted into the search field. These searches are especially useful the identification of stock images.

well-known networks. Therefore, the publicly available information on these platforms have to be taken into consideration.

Social Network Profiles are a helpful source to gather information about individuals and companies. LinkedIn and Xing profiles include information about a target's professional skills, connections with former employers, business relationships with colleagues or with other companies and of a person's education level (Albrechtslund, 2016). Twitter and Facebook have been abused by terrorist organizations such as ISIS to spread extremist propaganda. Incidents like these can impact the reputational risk of a merchant, should their associated accounts be involved in any way.

Interestingly, the total absence of social network profiles for an e-commerce merchant, associated director(s) and/or its ultimate beneficial owner(s) could also be an indication for a possible Transaction Laundering risk, since one would normally expect an online merchant to maintain social network profiles for advertising purposes.

Risk Indicator:	Social Network Profiles
Risk Indicator Classification:	Primary
Risk Category:	Reputation, Transaction Laundering
Connected Primary Risk Indicators:	none
Impact of the Risk Indicator:	reputational
Mitigation and Proceeding:	accept, decline
Common Location(s):	Website landing page Website contact Social Networks

2.3.23 Subscription Models

A card holder who participates in a subscription business model must pay a recurring fee to gain access to the offered services or products. Industries that commonly use this kind of model include software providers, fitness clubs, adult and dating content providers, video platforms or magazines. A common model on websites, known is the free trial. Here, a merchant provides either one tier of free content or restricted access for a short period of time (e.g. three days) before it converts into a full premium subscription. The overall business risk for merchants that are relying on prepaid subscription models is relatively high, as the risk of default applies to the full subscription period, until the service has been completely utilized or is expired. The longer the pre-paid subscription period runs (e.g. monthly, quarterly, yearly, etc.), the higher the financial exposure associated with it. Other factors which significantly increase chargeback risk, are unclear terms of subscription or cancellation procedures.

Risk Indicator:	Subscription Models
Risk Indicator Classification:	Primary
Risk Category:	Business, Chargeback, Financial
Connected Primary Risk Indicators:	none
Impact of the Risk Indicator:	financially
Mitigation and Proceeding:	control
Common Location(s):	Website terms & conditions Website payment page

2.3.24 Whois Privacy Services

A Whois privacy services offers a so-called 'Whois protection'. In most cases either the company offering Whois protection or a shell company (usually a Limited) is recorded as the owner of the domain. The aim is, to make it impossible for third parties to determine who actually owns and operates a website.

Particularly in e-commerce, the domain owner should coincide with the operator named in the corporate information on the website. In high-risk industries, like adult entertainment or dating, it has been quite common to use privacy services. This is due to the fact that the natural person who operates the website wants to obscure his/her connection to a website of this kind. This especially applies to affiliate websites.

When a simple e-commerce merchant makes use of a privacy service, it is cause for suspicion. Utilizing Whois protection to obfuscate website ownership therefore increases the Transaction Laundering risk.

Risk Indicator:	Whois Privacy Service
Risk Indicator Classification:	Primary
Risk Category:	Transaction Laundering
Connected Primary Risk Indicators:	none
Impact of the Risk Indicator:	financial, reputational
Mitigation and Proceeding:	amend, remove, accept
Common Location(s):	Whois information

2.3.25 Website Traffic

An important risk indicator during the underwriting process is the website traffic. To allocate website visitors and identify whether the website is even in use, two sources are recommended: Alexa[44] and Similarweb[45]. Both provide digital marketing services that collect website hits by internet users and stores

---
[44] www.alexa.com (12.08.2016).
[45] https://www.similarweb.com/ (12.08.2016).

these hits in a database. The data is analysed and calculated, which results in a ranking system, indicating the popularity of the company's website in terms of website visits. This information generally used by Marketing departments, but it is also quite useful to Underwriters. The Alexa scoring itself is quite abstract, but using it as a basis makes it possible to calculate the average visitors of a specific URL.

In this context, it is also recommended to review the website traffic history. Irregular or sudden increases of visitor traffic could be an indication for traffic buying. It is also interesting to verify whether identified user audience, matches geographically with the targeted markets of the legal entity. The website user traffic needs to be taken into account during any risk assessment, especially if the merchant has provided a processing history (for credit/debit card payments).

A website that has no traceable visitors at all should be considered as an increased Transaction Laundering risk, as this has been observed in connection with third party billing and miscoding.

Risk Indicator:	Website traffic
Risk Indicator Classification:	Primary
Risk Category:	Transaction Laundering
Connected Primary Risk Indicators:	none
Impact of the Risk Indicator:	financial, reputational
Mitigation and Proceeding:	accept, decline
Common Location(s):	Digital marketing services

2.4 Secondary Risk Indicators

2.4.1 Nominee Shareholders

A nominee shareholder is a person who holds shares in his own name on behalf of a third person (or the beneficiary) who, in reality, effectively owns and controls the relevant shares. He is the registered legal owner that holds the shares on trust of the beneficiary. The legal agreement between the nominee shareholder and the beneficiary is called a declaration of trust. Therein, the legal frame of the ownership are outlined: the legal owner (the nominee) has no rights whatsoever over the assets he holds or their income and he cannot act without instruction from the beneficiary.

Nominee shareholders are often used in combination with a company formation agency. A typical nominee shareholder can be identified if

a) Registered address of the merchant has been identified as being offered or used by a company formation agency

b) Shareholder is also the director of the corporation

c) Shareholder also holds multiple appointments in other corporations registered under the same address and active in different business areas.

A merchant that uses a nominee shareholder increases the money laundering risk for the merchant acquirer, as it obscures the true beneficiary owner (UBO). The true UBO needs to be identified and screened against sanction and PEP lists, in order to avoid the risk of unwillingly supporting illegal activities.

Risk Indicator:	Nominee Shareholder
Risk Indicator Classification:	Secondary
Risk Category:	AML
Connected Primary Risk Indicators:	Company Formation Agencies
Impact of the Risk Indicator:	financial, reputational
Mitigation and Proceeding:	accept or decline
Common Location(s):	Background Research on Address Identification of multiple Appointments

2.4.2 Third Party Billing & Miscoding

Third Party Billing and Miscoding are secondary risk indicators. Third Party Billing refers to the procedure where a merchant who does not hold the necessary license of a legal aggregator (e.g. e-money license) facilitates payments on behalf of a third party (another merchant). If the nature of the business is obscured, by utilizing a MCC[46] that does not relate to the business the merchant is engaged in, this practice is also considered miscoding. Miscoding is usually used by merchants who offer illegal services or products (e.g. drugs, pharmaceuticals, online gambling for U.S. and Turkish card holders etc.).[47]

As Third Party Billing and Miscoding often confuse the card holder and generates customer complaints, as the consumer receives a billing description which doesn't match with the website the shopper purchased his/her services/products from. In many cases, the researched merchant is offering goods or services of questionable quality, while the website has no visitors at all and could be considered inactive. Sometimes the terms and conditions contain information about an additional contracting party (e.g. another merchant is mentioned). A generic billing

---

[46] The **Merchant Category Code** (MCC or "Card Acceptor ID") is a four-digit number assigned by different credit card organizations when a merchant first starts accepting the respective form of payment. In the United States, it can be used to determine if a payment needs to be reported to the Internal Revenue Service for tax purposes. It is used to classify the activity of a merchant.

[47] Please compare the section Illegal Aggregation of this guide for more information.

descriptors and generic price points are also considered connected risk indicators.

Third Party Billing and Miscoding indications are Transaction Laundering risks that can have a massive impact on the financial risk of a merchant acquirer, due to possible associated fines due to non-compliance fees.

Risk Indicator:	Third Party Billing & Miscoding
Risk Indicator Classification:	Secondary
Risk Category:	Transaction laundering
Connected Primary Risk Indicators:	Customer complaints, Inactive website Intangible goods or services Generic billing descriptor Generic price points
Impact of the Risk Indicator:	financial
Mitigation and Proceeding:	amend, remove, control, decline
Common Location(s):	Website terms & conditions Customer complaints Website visitors

2.4.3 Transaction Load Balancing

The terms 'transaction load balancing', 'credit card load balancing' or 'merchant account load balancing' are known to the card industry since the early beginning of the internet and often have a negative connotation.[48] The term refers to a performance optimization tactic that provides fault-tolerance by splitting incoming transactions across several MIDs[49], in order to circumvent monitoring procedures of the merchant acquirer or card associations. In a load balancing case, the merchant contracts numerous acquirers to set up multiple merchant accounts. These accounts are then used to cascade transactions until a successful authorization is obtained. To be able to draw the right conclusion from this risk indicator, it is key to understand what the merchant's intentions are. Load balancing should not be viewed as negative by default. Currently, three different approaches to transaction load balancing can be observed:

a) Natural load balancing,
b) Strategic load balancing,
c) Fraudulent load balancing.

---

[48] More details about load balancing can be found in the MasterCard Revised Standards for Merchant and Submerchant Compliance (Global Operations Bulletin, December 1, 2014).
[49] A **merchant identification** (**MID**) number is a unique number assigned from the payment institution (most of the times the acquiring bank) to a merchant account to identify it throughout all processing activities.

Natural Load Balancing

Natural load balancing often occurs due to the fact that a merchant is active in several jurisdictions around the globe. To be able to provide card holders with a good after-sales service, a merchant might want to localize his billing descriptor to provide matching contact information for customers in that specific country. It is important to realize that domestic acquiring often benefits from higher approval rates, as some credit cards require an activation prior to using it abroad. In jurisdictions with very strong issuers who are also maintaining an acquiring branch, closed loop transactions can be used, which leads to a decrease in transaction fees. Despite conversion fees, some issuers also charge their card holders for using their credit card abroad, to the inconvenience of the cardholder.

Example:

The merchant "ABC Limited" is incorporated in the United Kingdom and is providing dating services to his customers via his website www.abc.com. When charging a UK card holder, the merchant might use his acquirer relationship in the United Kingdom to enable a domestic transaction and the billing descriptor that is displayed on the monthly credit card statement of the card holder reflects the details below:

ABC Limited / +44 123 45678910

> If the card holder is German, the merchant could utilize his German acquiring relationship and instead of displaying a UK based number in the billing descriptor, the merchant would want a German card holder to be able to get in touch with a German service representative and therefore the below billing descriptor is used:
>
> ABC Limited / +49 987 65432100
>
> As you can see, the merchant wants to offer a more convenient after-sales service by addressing customers in their native language. This leads to a form of natural transaction load balancing, because the transactions are distributed over multiple MIDs and merchant acquirers.

Natural load balancing should not be considered negative, as its intention is either to optimize interchange fees or to provide a more convenient customer service. Especially merchants that are operating on a global scale across various countries and languages are forced to provide localized contact details in order to optimize their chargeback prevention strategy.

Strategic Load Balancing

Strategic load balancing is mostly used by merchants that sell services/products which are considered as high-risk (i.e. emotional content, dating and gambling). Such businesses often have trouble staying below the given chargeback thresholds of the credit card associations. One of the reasons may be that they may be subject to (repetitive) fraud attacks that automatically increase the associated chargeback rate:

1. Affiliate fraud, and
2. "Friendly fraud" or chargeback fraud

High risk merchants often use affiliate networks to attract new customers. This can make them vulnerable to fraudulent affiliates, who use stolen credit card details on the merchant's website to simulate a real purchase and receive an affiliate commission. When the real cardholder receives his monthly statement and does not recognize the charge, he initiates a chargeback which increases the monthly chargeback threshold of the merchant.

"Friendly fraud" occurs, when a cardholder conducts a transaction with his own credit card and requests a chargeback from his issuing bank, after receiving the purchased service or product. Friendly fraud thrives in the digital products market where it is much easier for fraudsters to succeed. Attempts by the merchant to prove that the consumer received the purchased goods or services are very difficult.

Merchants involved in regular low-risk e-commerce business usually do not face such type of attacks and find it much easier to stay below the monthly chargeback thresholds. When merchants exceed their monthly chargeback limit, they are obliged to pay additional chargeback fees and penalties. Depending on the respective credit card brand, breaching these thresholds can lead to increasing fines. Therefore, some merchants use strategic load balancing as a way to avoid having to pay fines, ultimately resulting in losing their merchant account with their acquirer.

Strategic load balancing requires a lot of effort and money as multiple corporations and websites are needed to be able to stay below the thresholds. The merchant also needs to understand the basics of automated transaction routing, chargeback forecasting, transaction layering and the calculation of associated chargeback probabilities per layer. Strategic load balancing is mostly used by very experienced merchants that aim to keep a stable relationship with their acquirers and avoid the payment of fines. The merchant only processes a pre-calculated number of transactions per MID that is sufficient not to exceed the minimum number of chargebacks. In the case of strategic load balancing, it is very important that the associated billing descriptors are clearly communicated to the cardholder, so that he is able to recognize the charge. Otherwise this would cause even higher chargeback rates.

Example:

The merchant "ABC Limited" is providing dating services to his customers via his website www.abc.com. In this fictitious example, to be eligible for penalties, the merchant needs at least 100 chargebacks per month AND a chargeback-to-transaction ratio of 1 percent

The merchant is processing about 10.000 transactions per month in total, with an average chargeback-to-transaction ratio of 2 percent (200 chargebacks per month). As a result, he is paying monthly penalties and is putting his merchant account at risk. The merchant decides to set up two additional corporations with new websites/landing pages and provides these to his merchant acquirer.

After the two merchant accounts have been approved, he evaluates the average chargeback probability per transaction layer and then starts to route the transactions accordingly.

> Instead of processing all transactions through one single merchant account, he is now spreading it across three. Per merchant account he is processing 3.333 transactions per month. This in fact does not really reduce the chargeback to transaction ratio of 2 % as he still receives 66 chargebacks per merchant account and month, but he stays well below the necessary 100 chargebacks and therefore avoids being placed in any chargeback monitoring program. This way, he does not incur any penalties.

Setting up strategic load balancing only makes sense, if the costs associated with setting up and maintaining additional corporations and websites are lower than the costs of the monthly chargeback penalties.

Fraudulent Load Balancing

Load balancing is considered fraudulent, when its main purpose isn't the prevention of chargeback penalties (for slightly higher chargeback-to-transaction ratios), but the abuse of merchant accounts for processing unauthorized transactions (e.g. stolen cards). Indications for fraudulent load balancing attempts are the use of very generic billing descriptors that cannot be tracked to any specific product or website, for example "Healthy Food /

United Kingdom" or multiple customer complaints relating to unauthorized charges.[50] In addition, analyzing transactions with a focus on authorization declines can also be a good indicator for fraudulent load balancing, especially when the number of declines for lost or stolen cards exceeds the common average.

Strategic and fraudulent transaction load balancing increase the associated business and chargeback risk (chargeback risk on volume basis, not on count) for the associated merchant acquirers. In cases of fraudulent load balancing, the fraud risk and Transaction Laundering risk is considered as very high, as possible penalties by the card associations might be pending. Appropriate transaction monitoring controls need to be put in place, in order to control and identify the purpose and nature of the conducted transactions.

Risk Indicator:	Transaction Load Balancing
Risk Indicator Classification:	Secondary
Risk Category:	Business, Chargeback, Fraud, Transaction Laundering
Connected Primary Risk Indicators:	Mirror Websites, Multiple Corporations, Inactive Websites, Multiple Billing Descriptors, Support Websites
Impact of the Risk Indicator:	financial, reputational
Mitigation and Proceeding:	accept or decline
Common Location(s):	none, as it is a secondary risk indicator

---

[50] An interesting case of fraudulent load balancing is discussed in the article "FTC How-To Guide for Ripping Off Card Brands on http://www.pymnts.com/news/2014/ftc-how-to-guide-for-ripping-off-card-brands/ (03.08.2016).

2.5 Starting the Investigation

Looking up the term 'online investigation' with a search engine, will result in hundreds of results, all giving different ideas, paradigms and structures to facilitate an online investigation. This Best Practice Guide is following the framework of the "Investigative Risk Analysis" (Chmiel, 2010) as taught in the "Certified High-Risk Underwriter" Course of the Web Shield Academy.[51]

2.6 Using the Investigative Risk Analysis

The Investigative Risk Analysis can be summarized in four consecutive steps:

1. Understand the Business,
2. Collect Data,
3. Research the Data,
4. Analyze the Data and Conclude.

During each step of the investigation, the Underwriter is encouraged to identify the associated primary and secondary risk

---

[51] For more information about the Web Shield Academy, please refer to the appendix of this Best Practice Guide or visit **www.webshield.com**.

indicators as outlined in section 2.3.1 and the following instructions.

2.6.1 Understand the Business

It might appear obvious that it is necessary to understand a merchant's business first, but this essential step should not be underestimated. It contains various elements which should be taken into consideration at the beginning of every investigation.

Product / Service

Information about offered product or service can be drawn from various sources, such as

- a) Provided documents (e.g. the certificate of incorporation, the memorandum of articles, the business description in the merchant contract, a provided business plan), and/or
- b) Retrieved documents (e.g. credit reports or investigation reports), and/or
- c) The merchant's web presence (e.g. the merchant's website, connected social network profiles, online job offerings, customer feedback, online advertisements).

In order to gain a deeper understanding of the products and/or services a merchant offers, it is recommended to answer the following investigation questions. These help to calculate and evaluate the associated risks:

- What product or service is the researched merchant offering?
- Can the business offerings be considered high-risk, high brand risk or even illegal?
- Is it easy to understand the offering?[52]
- Does the offering require any kind of special licensing (e.g. gambling operators, pharmacies)?
- Does the merchant offer tangible or intangible products?
- Does the product or service require any kind of verifications or are there any restrictions (e.g. local or age restrictions, customer KYC procedures)?
- Does the product or service require any kind of registration with the card associations (e.g. airlines, or MRP registration for high-risk businesses)?

---

[52] If an Underwriter, whose daily business consists of the quick evaluation of many different business models is having a hard time understanding an offering, this should be considered a red flag. If a trained Underwriter does not fully comprehend a merchant's offerings, the average customer will probably be even more clueless.

These questions do not represent a complete list, but they can give the investigator an idea on how to approach the research. After answering the above questions, the first risk indicators can be identified. It is strongly recommended to document these as part of the investigation and for further analysis.

> **Example:**
>
> Following the questions above, the Underwriter reviews the provided business plan and merchant website. She concludes that the merchant is located in Malta and is operating an online casino.
>
> Due to the classification of various card associations, the business would be classified as high risk (High-Risk / High Brand Risk Indicator).
>
> As the merchant is located in a jurisdiction that requires a gambling license to offer these kind of services, the risk indicator 'Licensed Business' can be drawn.
>
> Operating a licensed gambling platform in Malta requires the merchant to have a suitable KYC procedure for customers in place, as minors are prohibited from participating. The risk indicators 'Customer KYC required' and 'Age verification necessary' could be drawn from this fact.
>
> Finally, the investigated business would be classified under the MCC 7995 for gambling and therefore a registration with

the card associations would be necessary (Registration with Card Association).[53]

From simply understanding the service offerings of the merchant in question, the below risk indicators could be drawn:

- High-Risk Business,

- Licensed Business,

- Customer KYC required,

- Age Verification necessary,

- Registration with Card Association.

Sales Procedure

Another important element to investigate, is the type of customers the merchant is targeting and how? It is vital to understand how and where transactions are generated, as here indications for fraud or deception can be identified.

---

[53] A registration of such a merchant could be necessary in the MasterCard Registration Program (MRP).

There are various sources of information that can be used to find out how a merchant is targeting customers. The vast majority of that information can be retrieved by merely researching for the merchant name or the associated website. In addition to that, online research tools for the identification of user traffic[54] and user sources (e.g. backlinks) should be utilized.

To understand a merchant's sales procedure, it is recommended to answer the investigation questions below:

- Are the terms of service and associated charges clearly visible to the customer?
- Are any kind of deceptive marketing methods being utilized by the merchant?
- Is there any kind of customer feedback (e.g. complaints related to a deceptive subscription model, articles, blogs or discussions in bulletin boards about the product, etc.)?
- Are social network profiles of the merchant available and are they used to advertise products or services?

---

[54] e. g. **www.alexa.com**, or **www.similarweb.com**; reviewed on May, 16th, 2016.

- Does the merchant's website allow or actively disallow the indexing of content (e.g. disallowing search engines from indexing the site through the robots.txt file, embedding product or contact information in images)?
- In advertising his services, is the merchant using a call center, email marketing or an affiliate network?
- Does the website have user traffic, where is the customer audience geography, or is it a business that does not even require a website, as it is operated via a call center or mobile application (e.g. remote PC services)?
- Where the merchant is located and is he offering his products or services only locally? If he operates internationally, could there be issues due to cross-border shipping?

Again, answering the above questions and identifying the associated risk indicators will further help the investigator to understand the merchant in detail.

> **Example:**
>
> After reviewing the website of the gambling operator, the Underwriter identifies an affiliate network. After conducting research on www.alexa.com regarding the website visitors and the associated customer audience geography, the Underwriter notes that 90 percent of the associated website users

originate from Malta and another 10 percent from other countries. In addition, a very low global rank scoring is issued from which the Underwriter draws the conclusion that the website has quite a respective number of visitors. After reviewing the website history with the help of the Waybackmachine (www.archive.org), the Underwriter finds out that the website is operating since at least 2012. The background research of the merchant reveals various discussions in online bulletin boards about the associated loyalty program and a few advertisements on blogs.

The below risk indicators can be drawn, from simply understanding the sales procedure of the merchant:

- Affiliate Network utilized,
- Customer Feedback identified,
- Online Ads identified.

Content and/or Fulfillment Control

The last step to understand a merchant's business, is to know who is in charge of the content, the product, the service and the associated fulfilment, as this also has a direct impact on the possible risks and necessary monitoring procedures.

This step can be considered the hardest part of an investigation, because much of the necessary information is not publicly available. Normally, only the merchant or the website operators possess this specialized knowledge. Though this may be the case, sometimes the information about implemented content or fulfilment controls can be retrieved from the terms of service, where the Underwriter retrieves which party is in charge for what kind of fulfilment, if any kind of specific monitoring procedures are set into place and who has the final control over the content. In cases where users are capable of uploading and sharing digital content or are allowed to offer their own products and services, this is crucial information.

To understand the content or fulfilment control, it is recommended to answer the investigation questions below:

- Are users able to upload or share digital content?
- Are users able to offer products or services themselves?
- What kind of monitoring or approval procedures are in place, if user generated content is identified?
- Can the business be considered a likely target for the upload or sale of illegal products or services?
- Is it clear to the customer who is in charge of the service fulfillment (e.g. is there a fulfilment center involved)?

- Are there any kind of third party billing indications (e.g. are there indications for the merchant facilitating transactions on behalf of a third party)?

Of course, there are many more questions that should be asked here. Nevertheless, the current list can already supply the investigator with key risk indicators that help the Underwriter during the Onboarding and Customer Acceptance phase.

> **Example:**
>
> After setting up a test account on the website of the gambling operator, the Underwriter identifies an online bulletin board in the member area of the platform. The terms of service state that all new postings require a formal approval by the moderator. The terms of service further outline that the gambling operator is monitoring the transactions of the customers regarding fraudulent patterns. In addition, the merchant name and address is mentioned as the only entity on the website. The Underwriter concludes that the named corporation is solely in charge of all associated payment transactions.
>
> From understanding the content and fulfilment control procedure of the merchant an Underwriter could draw the following risk indicator:
>
> - Bulletin Board utilized

It is important to understand that answering the question of who is in control of the content has a direct impact on the probability of violations and any possible connected fines.

2.6.2 Collect Data

Now that the Underwriter understands the merchant's offerings, the sales procedures and who has the content and fulfillment control, the data collection procedure starts. Depending on the jurisdiction and the respective regulation, the accessible documents and sources at hand may vary. This Best Practice Guide is focusing on the standard documents that are required in compliance with the rules and regulations of the card associations. These documents are:

Merchant Agreement or Merchant Contract

The merchant agreement or merchant contract contains the general merchant information that should correlate with the information drawn from the incorporation documents.

In addition, the merchant agreement can also contain additional contact details. This includes data such as

- Doing business name (DBA),
- Phone and fax numbers,
- Email addresses,
- Additional contact persons,
- VAT number,
- Discount rate,
- Currencies and payments brands,
- Requested billing descriptor,
- Average ticket size, the average and maximum delivery period (or service period), as well as the forecasted monthly turnover with the requested payment methods.

Corporate Documents

Depending on the jurisdiction of the merchant, various corporate documents are available. In this Best Practice Guide we are focusing on the most common documents which would be

- Certificate of Incorporation or Current Appointments Report, and
- Shareholder Certificate.

No matter how these documents are referred to, in general they contain the below information that should be collected for the next research phase:

- Name of the corporation,
- Registered number of the corporation,
- Date of incorporation,
- List of appointed directors and secretaries,
- Registered address of the corporation,
- List of shareholders.

Website

The websites of a merchant are an essential source for additional information and data that should be collected and researched. In this case, the Underwriter is not only looking for regular data but also additional details and data that can be used in the research:

- Additional email addresses,
- Phone numbers,
- Fax numbers,
- Additional addresses,

- Additional entities or corporations (e.g. fulfillment centers or otherwise connected entities),
- Additional websites (e.g. if the merchant is referring to a support website[55]),
- Details about the members of the management team,
- Billing descriptor,
- Information about affiliate networks,
- Customer testimonials,
- Details about the cancellation or refund procedure (e.g. return merchandise authorization or RMA)[56],
- Shipping details (shipping period and restricted countries),
- Regulation/licensing number[57],
- Specific images of the associated directors (if available), the office building (if available), or the product(s) itself.

In order to gather all the aforementioned elements, it is recommended to simulate a checkout procedure or to sign up for the

---

[55] Compare section 3.1.2 of the Fundamentals of Card-not-Present Merchant Acceptance Edition 2016 (2015).
[56] Compare section 2.3.18 in this book.
[57] A regulation or licensing number is necessary for merchants that operate in a regulated industry such as pharmacies, gambling operators or financial service providers.

service to be actually capable of retrieving the desired information. In many cases, a sign-up or checkout process needs to be initiated to get to the payment page of a website where the billing descriptor is displayed.

In addition to the website itself, the Underwriter should review all the associated Metadata. Relating to the website, this mostly means the source code, IP address and Whois information.[58] To summarize, the following information should be collected from a merchant:

- Meta keywords (found in the source code),
- Additional URLs on the IP address and/or the IP range (from a reverse IP analysis),
- Additional names and/or corporations (Whois),
- Additional phone numbers and fax numbers (Whois),
- Additional addresses (Whois), and
- Additional email addresses (Whois).

The data collection phase is quite labor-intensive, especially if the merchant operates several entities across different countries

---

[58] The procedure on how these details can be retrieved are outlined in the chapters "Whois Information", "Reverse IP Analysis" and "Source Code Analysis" of the section "Online Tools and Sources of Information" of this book.

and multiple websites. Nevertheless, years of investigations have proven that it is often the little details that allow the Underwriter to see the full picture.

2.6.3 Research the Data

The upcoming chapter will focus primarily on the previously outlined data, how it should be utilized in a comprehensive investigation and what resources should be used in the process:

MERCHANT NAME / DBA

- Research the merchant name with search engines,
- Identify additional merchant related contact details (e.g. phone numbers, email addresses),
- Identify customer feedback (e.g. complaints) relating to the name,
- Identify and review fraud or scam warnings relating to the name,
- Identify and review negative/positive news relating to the name,
- Identify and review entries on blacklists and/or sanction lists,
- Identify and review additional websites,

- Identify and review social network profiles (e.g. Facebook, LinkedIn),
- Identify other related merchants or entities (e. g. parent or sister corporations, subsidiaries, etc.),
- Compare to the provided incorporation documents.

Sources:

- Search Engines,
- Corporate Registries (online),
- Regulatory Websites (if merchant operates in a regulated industry),
- Whois (Reverse Whois),
- Blacklists,
- Sanction Lists,
- Credit Bureaus.

Additional research needs to be conducted, if one or multiple of the below indicators have been identified:

- Additional merchant controlled/operated websites have been identified,

- Merchant related entities (e. g. subsidiaries) have been identified.

Merchant Address

- Research the merchant address with search engines,
- Identify additional merchants or entities that are located at the researched address,
- Identify customer feedback (e. g. complaints) relating to the address,
- Identify and review fraud or scam warnings relating to the address,
- Identify and review negative/positive news relating to the address,
- Identify and review entries on blacklists and/or sanction lists,
- Identify and review additional websites operated under the registered address,
- Identify if the address is operated by an incorporation service, mail forwarding service or a virtual office operator,
- Match the address with the provided incorporation documents.

Sources:

- Search Engines,
- Corporate Registries (online),
- Blacklists,
- Sanction Lists.

Additional research needs to be conducted if one or multiple of the below indicators have been identified:

- Entities registered under the same address have been identified,
- Websites operated by entities registered under the same address.

VAT and Incorporation Number

- Research the VAT and incorporation number with search engines,
- Identify additional merchants or entities operating under the same numbers,

- Verify validity of the VAT[59] and Incorporation Number[60].

Sources:

- Search Engines,
- Corporate Registries (online),
- Regulatory Websites.

Additional research needs to be conducted if one or multiple of the below indicators have been identified:

- Entities have been identified that are operating under the same VAT and/or incorporation number,
- The provided VAT and/or incorporation number is invalid or a mismatch.

Director/Secretary/Ultimate Beneficial Owner and other additional contacts

- Research the name(s) with search engines,

---

[59] e. g. **http://ec.europa.eu/taxation_customs/vies/?locale=en**, (29.06.2016).
[60] e. g. **https://opencorporates.com/**, (29.06.2016).

- Identify additional related contact details (e.g. phone numbers, email addresses),
- Identify and review fraud or scam warnings relating to the name(s),
- Identify and review negative/positive news relating to the name(s),
- Identify and review entries on blacklists and/or sanction lists,
- Identify and review social network profiles (e.g. Facebook, LinkedIn),
- Identify and review additional websites registered to the name(s),
- Identify other related merchants or entities (e.g. multiple director appointments),
- Compare to the provided incorporation documents.

Sources:

- Search Engines,
- Corporate Registries (online),
- Whois (Reverse Whois),
- Blacklists,
- Sanction Lists.

Additional research needs to be conducted if one or multiple of the below indicators have been identified:

- Additional websites registered to the name(s) have been identified,
- Other related entities (e.g. multiple director appointments) that have been identified.

Billing Descriptor

- Research the billing descriptor(s) with search engines,
- Identify additional related websites that might also be connected to this billing descriptor (e.g. if the billing descriptor is also found in the footer, the terms and conditions or the payment page of an additional website),
- Identify and review fraud or scam warnings relating to the billing descriptor(s),
- Identify and review negative/positive news relating to the billing descriptor(s),
- Identify and review entries on blacklists,
- Identify other related merchants or entities (e.g. other merchants that are using the same billing descriptor which would be considered third party billing indications).

Sources:

- Search Engines,
- Blacklists,
- Sanction Lists.

Additional research needs to be conducted if one or multiple of the below indicators have been identified:

- Additional websites using the same billing descriptor(s) have been identified,
- Other related entities have been identified.

Websites

- Research the website with search engines,
- Research the website with a content web crawler (for the identification of BRAM or GBPP violations),
- Identify additional website related contact details (e.g. phone numbers, email addresses),
- Identify customer feedback (e.g. complaints) relating to the website,
- Identify and review fraud or scam warnings relating to the website,

- Identify and review negative/positive news relating to the website,
- Identify and review entries on blacklists,
- Identify and review additional websites,
- Identify and review social network profiles (e.g. Facebook, LinkedIn, etc.),
- Identify other related merchants or entities (e.g. parent or sister corporations, subsidiaries).

Sources:

- Search Engines,
- Web Crawler,
- Whois (Reverse Whois),
- Blacklists.

Additional research needs to be conducted if one or multiple of the below indicators have been identified:

- Additional websites controlled/operated by the same merchant have been identified,
- Illegal products or services have been detected (BRAM or GBPP violations),
- Other website related Entities have been identified.

Contact Details (Email, Phone, Fax)

- Research the contact details with search engines,
- Identify additional merchants, entities or websites operating with the same contact details (e.g. if the Whois directory is displaying the same details),
- Identify and review fraud or scam warnings as well as customer complaints relating to the contact details,
- Identify and review entries on blacklists,
- Verify validity of the email address[61].

Sources:

- Search Engines,
- Whois (Reverse Whois),
- Blacklists.

Additional research needs to be conducted if one or multiple of the below indicators have been identified:

- Entities have been identified that are operating under the same contact details,

---

[61] There are various online tools that can be used to verify if an email address is valid such as **http://email-checker.net/** or **http://verify-email.org/** (28.07.2016).

- The identified or provided contact details are invalid.

Researching the collected data often leads to the collection of additional data that needs to be researched again – a recursive process. This stage of the underwriting process is actually a combination of data research and additional data collection and therefore needs to be repeated until no additional data can been found. After the Underwriter has gathered all the above information, he/she can move to the next step.

2.6.4 Analyze the Data and Conclude

Now that all data has been collected and researched and the primary risk indicators have been identified, the investigator has to thoroughly analyze the findings, deduce secondary risk indicators in order to come to a final conclusion. The identified primary investigative risk indicators have to be classified under the risk categories outlined in section 2.1.

> **Example:**
>
> The remote PC service operator "Sample IT Limited" is maintaining the website www.samplehelp.com. The Underwriter identified several customer complaints for the phone number, complaints relating to various unrecognizable billing descriptors, two additional merchant related websites where

one can be considered a processing site and the second a support website, as well as a mirror website, operated by a merchant registered at the same address as "Sample IT Limited". The Underwriter classifies the **primary** investigative risk indicators under the categories:

- **Business Risks** (Remote PC Service, Mirror Websites)

- **AML Risks**

- **Reputation Risks** (Customer Complaints detected)

- **Financial Risks**

- **Transaction Laundering Risks** (Additional Merchant Related URLs detected, Support Websites)

- **Brand Risks**

- **Chargeback Risks** (generic billing descriptor, multiple billing descriptors)

- **Fraud Risks**

- **Other Risks**

In the above example, each primary risk indicator is only used once and does not occur in multiple categories (e.g. a generic billing descriptor is increasing the chargeback risk and the Transaction Laundering risk). It is up to the Underwriter, the underwriting policy or the used risk assessment methodology to either place a risk indicator under several categories or choose the one where the indicator has the highest impact.

During the next step, the associated secondary risk indicators have to be identified. As demonstrated in the section "Secondary Risk Indicators" in this guide, these are based on the connection of at least two primary risk indicators.

> **Example:**
>
> From reviewing all associated primary risk indicators, the Underwriter identifies a secondary risk indicator: Transaction Load Balancing. She draws this conclusion from the fact that various mirror and support websites have been detected and the merchant is using multiple billing descriptors. All of these primary risk indicators can be connected to Transaction Load Balancing. The Underwriter then classifies the **secondary** investigative risk indicators under the risk categories:
>
> - **Business Risks** (Remote PC Service, Mirror Websites, Transaction Load Balancing)
> - **AML Risks**

- **Reputation Risks** (Customer Complaints detected)

- **Financial Risks**

- **Transaction Laundering Risks** (Additional Merchant Related URLs detected, Support Websites)

- **Brand Risks**

- **Chargeback Risks** (generic billing descriptor)

- **Fraud Risks**

- **Other Risks**

In this example, the Underwriter has to take into consideration all other risk indicators that can be salvaged from other sources, e.g. a higher financial exposure due to long subscription terms relating to additional websites or a bad credit rating from a credit bureau. All risk indicators have to be taken into consideration in order to come to a balanced risk assessment

Depending on the internal policy of the merchant acquirer, this risk overview should be analyzed both quantitatively and qualitatively

Some examples of a quantitative analysis:

- Total number of primary risk indicators per risk category.
- Total number of secondary risk indicators.
- Individual weighting of the identified risk indicators.
- Individual weighting of the utilized risk categories.
- Calculated or forecasted financial risk exposure.

By adding a quantitative approach, the Underwriter can make merchant applications comparable to each other on the basis of a total scoring.

Based on the risk overview, the Underwriter is now able to determine the next necessary steps: Mitigating potential risks. Some risks can be easily removed (e.g. a specific product is violating the prohibited product list and therefore needs to be removed from the merchant's website), others have to be amended (e.g. the merchant's website is lacking a privacy policy), controlled (e.g. by putting certain transaction monitoring procedures in place), covered (e.g. a very high financial exposure is identified and covered with additional collaterals), or accepted (e.g. the merchant is registered under the address of a known incorporation service). At the end of this process an acquiring bank can determine whether the merchant can be boarded and the MIDs issued, if the merchant needs to make amendments first, or if the application needs to be declined.

The following preliminary questions can help an Underwriter to come to a balanced decision:

- Has enough proof been found, that the researched merchant is really conducting the business that he claims to run and is it clear who is in control of the content, the services or the products?

- Are the merchant's business model and the associated risks acceptable from a legal point of view, concerning the rules and regulations of the card associations (e.g. website compliance, the nature of goods and services offered as well as proper licensing) and the internal policies of the acquirer (e. g. prohibited products lists)?

- Did you identify risk indicators which cannot simply be removed, amended, controlled or covered and therefore could be accepted? Is this compliant and in line with the internal policies of the acquirer (in other words the 'Risk Appetite') and have the potential financial or reputational risks been fully considered?

- Is the examined business model vulnerable to specific forms of fraud attacks (e. g. affiliate transaction cleansing)?
- Can the associated financial exposure be accurately calculated or predicted and if so, can sufficient collaterals be imposed to cover chargeback and refund risks?[62]

After answering the above questions, it is recommended to conclude an investigation with a summary Report, which also contains the recommendations for further actions.

2.7 Summarizing the Investigation

When an online investigation is complete, written documentation of all gathered evidence has to be provided. This is necessary for record keeping purpose and it supports evidence for the final verdict. Furthermore, a complete documentation is important for the following reasons:

---

[62] In the case of high-risk businesses, the potential for non-compliance penalties by the card associations should also be considered.

1. Document for action

In some cases, control and prevention measures a merchant acquirer has to put in place will only be instituted in response to a written report.

2. Record of performance

The Investigation Summary documents the magnitude of the identified risks and justifies necessary actions. It should include all steps undertaken by the Underwriter. The comprehensiveness of the Investigation Summary should reflect the complexity of the investigation. This accurately documents possible problems and also clearly illustrates the sources utilized to undertake the investigation.

3. Evidence in legal cases

An Investigation Summary must be written objectively, honestly and fairly by the Risk Professional. Information in these investigations is frequently used in legal actions such as court cases, police investigations or non-compliance situations with card schemes. Thus, it is very important that a record exists that accurately documents events in a timely manner to aid in any legal investigations that might ensue.

4. Enhancement investigation quality

The process of writing a report and reviewing data in written form may result in new insights. It could precipitate new questions before a conclusion is reached. The more investigations one writes up, the better the understanding of the processes and results.

The investigation summary should specify into great details which risk indicators need to be

a) Removed,

b) Amended,

c) Controlled

d) Covered.

The risk covered by an acquirer's risk appetite should also be outlined in detail. Finally, the report should conclude how to proceed with the merchant application and whether the Underwriter considers rejecting the merchant on base of the identified risk indicators.

Sample Investigation Summary:

The merchant is offering furniture on his website(s). The price comparison identified irregularities. During the investigation, the product has been researched. Clear indications for counterfeit goods have been detected during the research. The merchant is located in a country where the online sale of the alleged illegitimate product does violate applicable country laws. Details about the identified content violations can be found in the appendix of this report.

The merchant seems to be registered by an incorporation service. It is assumed that this merchant is/was a shell (or shelf) company. This conclusion has been drawn due to the identification of an incorporation service. No recent customer complaints have been detected during the background research.

Indications for the appointment of a nominee director/shareholder have been detected. This assumption is based on the fact that the appointed director has been identified as having multiple appointments with multiple entities in different sectors, all registered under the same address (or two/three different addresses).

A moderate credit rating has been provided by the credit bureau. A medium credit limit (between 1.000 EUR and 25.000 EUR) has been detected. The international risk has been classified as B (low risk). A very high financial exposure has been calculated for this merchant due to very long deliver times (< 6 months).

> The merchant is using a privacy service for the Whois entry of his URL(s). The research has detected that the merchant is also providing a mobile app. This needs to be considered when setting up the appropriate risk controls.
>
> Due to the identification of the sale of counterfeit goods in countries where the online sale violates applicable laws, the merchant application has been declined.

Considering the variety of potential primary and secondary risk indicators, the outlined investigation strategy should not be static. It is an ongoing process. The Underwriter needs to stay up-to-date and he/she has to be familiar with new business models, cardholder behavior, fraud attacks or regulatory changes. Practical experience with this kind of investigation strategy can be obtained at the Certified High-Risk Underwriter Courses which are offered by the Web Shield Academy.[63]

---

[63] Please compare section "Recommended Courses" for more information.

3. Online Tools and Sources of Information

In the previous edition of the Fundamentals of Card-Not-Present Merchant Acceptance (2015) a total number of 16 online resources were reviewed in detail. The provided descriptions were mainly focusing on the detection of additional merchant related details, how internet research is conducted and how the infamous Dark Net can be utilized during the course of an investigation.

This new edition will add resources primarily aimed at the issue of aggregation and Transaction Laundering. This helps Underwriters to identify unknown websites and to understand where a merchant's customers are actually coming from. Understanding traffic sources is key if the Underwriter wants to understand the utilized sales channels.

3.1   SSL Certificate

Secure Sockets Layer (SSL) Certificates are data files that digitally bind a cryptographic key to keep sensitive information sent across the Internet encrypted. Information sent across the Internet is passed from computer to computer to get to a destination server. Without the SSL certificate, any computer between the sender and the destination server could read the passed on information. It is mainly used to secure credit card and banking details, data transfers, usernames and passwords and other sensitive information.[64]

The encrypted information can only be returned to a readable format with the proper decryption key. SSL certificates may also provide authentication to ensure that the information is transferred to the correct server instead of a malicious or compromised server.

It is easy to verify whether or not a SSL certificate is installed on a web server. Just check the web browser line. The application protocol known as HTTP will change to HTTPS. The "S" stands for secure.

Without SSL - http://webshieldltd.com/

With SSL – https://login.webshieldltd.com/

---

[64] https://www.globalsign.com/en/ssl-information-center/what-is-an-ssl-certificate/ (26.08.2016).

The SSL certificate can also be verified by inspecting an element via the browser console, for example if content is implemented in an inline frame (also known as iframe).

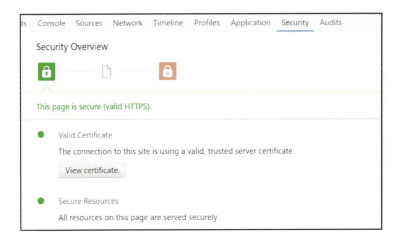

The SSL certificate is an important PCI compliance requirement. These requirements can be found in the Visa Europe Operating Regulations (2015) under point 4.12.C - Data Protection Methods.

> "An Acquirer has to ensure that its Electronic Commerce Merchants offer Cardholders a Data Protection Method (such as 3-D Secure or Secure Socket Layer (SSL))."

The SSL certificate can also be used to identify additional domains with the help of the Subject Alternative Name field. Subject Alternative Names (SANs) are used to secure multiple sites across different domains/subdomains. Just click on "View certificate" in the web browser console or on the green padlock icon (under "Details" in the web browser line).

The following screenshot[65] shows the Subject Alternative Names extension that lists additional domains/subdomains secured by the certificate.

---

[65] SANs secured by certificate on https://webfitnesscentral.com/vigor (24.08.2016).

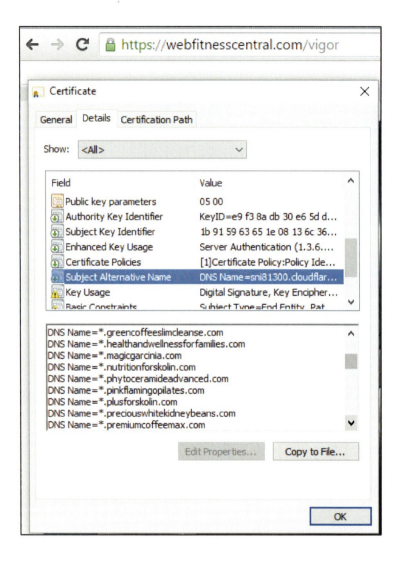

3.2 Traffic Source

To paint a picture of the various sources of web traffic associated with a particular website, an Underwriter should know both the Audience Geography distribution as well as the most important Referral URLs.

Audience Geography data describes the geographical location of all the visitors during the last month, by using **Geolocation**. Audience Geography data is mostly used for marketing purposes to tailor content and advertisements to audiences in specific regions.

Digital marketing services[66], IP-address and BIN checks can be used to gather these details to verify potential mismatches pertaining to the targeted website visitor's location and the actual website visitor's location; for example, a Dutch language website, attracting mostly visitors from Spain.

---

[66] Recommended services for Audience Geography, referral URL and traffic source data are http://www.alexa.com/ and https://www.similarweb.com/

In addition, Audience Geography data can be used to verify if products or services are offered within jurisdiction in which these products or services are prohibited or regulated.

The following sample screenshot display the Audience Geography of an online gambling operator.

🇺🇸 United States	**85.56%**
🇬🇧 United Kingdom	1.75%
🇩🇪 Germany	1.74%
🇭🇺 Hungary	1.57%
🇯🇵 Japan	1.28%

See 27 more countries

Over 85% of the website visitors are located in the United States, where online gambling is prohibited and transactions from U.S.

cardholders coded with the MCC for online gambling, 7995, are blocked by the issuing banks.

Another important clue to the traffic source of a website are the detected Referral URLs. These are the URLs of the websites on which a visitor clicked on a link in order to arrive at the investigated website. Identifying these URLs helps the investigator understand the sources of website visitors.

The mentioned Digital Marketing Services Alexa and SimliarWeb also offer this information. As an example: The domain tzarmedia.com, an entertainment provider offering access to digital content such as games, music, movies and books, generates over 60 percent of traffic from referral URLs[67].

---

[67] 2016-08-12 https://www.similarweb.com/website/tzarmedia.com#referrals

The top referring sites are kickasstorrentsan.com, torrentz.eu, 123movies.to, opensubtitles.org and ufindmedia.com. These sites are used for the free distribution (intellectual property right infringement) of digital content. The Top Destination Sites of tzarmedia's visitors, offer similar content. Ignoring the fact that the content offered on the referral sites is probably illegal, the question arises why someone would go from a free content site to a fee-based site and afterwards to an additional site which offers the same content.

An Underwriter could conclude that the operator of tzarmedia.com does not offer the content, advertised on the referral sites, at all.

Traffic Sources offer information on how website traffic is generated. SimilarWeb, for example, distinguishes six categories:

- **Direct**, traffic generated due to direct access of the site (e.g. URL input in browser line),
- **Referrals**, traffic generated with the help of referral sites,
- **Search**, traffic generated by search engine results,
- **Social**, traffic generated by social network sites,
- **Mail**, traffic generated via email marketing,

- **Display**, traffic generated via display advertisements, e.g. pop-up ads and website banners,

On a standard e-commerce website, it would be suspicious if the traffic source would only be Direct. Usually, only search engines and very well-known websites have a high direct traffic value (e.g. bing.com with 68%[68] and Google.com with 69%[69]).

---

[68] https://www.similarweb.com/website/bing.com#overview (12.08.2016).
[69] https://www.similarweb.com/website/google.com#overview (12.08.2016).

4. Aggregation

Aggregation, also referred to as Transaction Laundering, is widely considered the new trend in payment fraud. Consequently, the industry is targeting this bog challenge. In July, 2015, MasterCard released its Revised Standards for the Business Risk Assessment and Mitigation (BRAM) Program, which explicitly focuses on Transaction Laundering.

Before specifying different forms of Transaction Laundering, it is necessary to understand that Transaction Laundering is actually a part of Aggregation. Aggregation can be divided into "Compliant Aggregation", "Incompliant Aggregation" and "Illegal Aggregation".

4.1 Compliant Aggregation

A compliant aggregator is complying with the rules and regulations of the card associations. Compliant aggregators aggregate with the permission of the associated merchant acquirer.[70] Typical examples are Internet Payment Service Providers (IPSPs)[71], Payment Facilitators (PFs)[72], E-wallets or Marketplaces such as www.amazon.com. Such aggregators are required to pass through a formal approval process, either with the merchant acquirer or with the card associations, as part of the onboarding process, after which monitoring is outsourced to the aggregator.

4.2 Incompliant Aggregation

Incompliant Aggregation takes place when payment processing from a website - unknown to the PSP or acquirer - takes place, operated by a merchant that does not offer or promote illegal services or products.

---

[70] An "Internet Payment Service Provider", shortened form "IPSP" (Grabe, 2006), or "Payment Facilitator", shortened form "PF" (Worthington, 1995), is an online entity that is not a direct member of a credit card organization and contracts with an acquirer to acquire merchants on his behalf and to provide online payment services to a sponsored merchant.

[71] The expression "Internet Payment Service Provider" (**IPSP**) is mostly used in the terms of the card association **Visa**.

[72] The expression "Payment Facilitator" (PF) is mostly used in the terms of the card association **MasterCard**.

> **Example:**
>
> The merchant Test Limited is processing www.baby.com. He is also selling the same products on www.baby.org but this website is unknown to the acquirer

When it comes to incompliant aggregation there is no assumption that the merchant is intentionally misleading or misinforming the merchant acquirer.

> **Example:**
>
> A merchant that is selling clothing online also opened an online shop for shoes and is processing this through the same merchant account, without notifying the merchant acquirer.

Although this type of aggregation is not compliant with card scheme regulations, neither with the boarding and processing procedures of merchant acquirers, the associated financial and reputational risk is considered negligible. This type of aggregation doesn't pose a serious threat to the acquirer, as no illegal product or service is involved, and therefore rarely leads to actions by card associations.

This changes, as soon as a high-risk business is involved, as the acquirer might have to register the processed website with the card associations. MasterCard, for example, requires the registration of gambling MCCs with the MasterCard MRP program.

> **Example:**
>
> A merchant operating a casino website, also operates a second online casino and is processing these transactions through the same merchant account without notifying the merchant acquirer.

In this case, the financial and reputational risk for the merchant acquirer is significant. The merchant is operating a business considered to be high-risk. All operated websites must be registered with the card associations. In addition, the acquirer is required to re-assess the second website and compare the games offered with the license of the operator.

4.3 Illegal Aggregation

Illegal Aggregation refers to the fraudulent practice of a merchant who is aggregating transactions from a different merchant or website under his own merchant account, without the permission of the merchant acquirer. It most frequently involves the sale of an illegal product or service. Illegal aggregation challenges merchant acquirers and IPSPs, as they lead to thorough investigations by the card associations. If their investigations conclude that illegally aggregated payment transactions have been processed, this results in heavy penalties imposed by the card associations. In this context, it is crucial to understand that illegal aggregation can be categorized as:

a) Transaction Laundering without Miscoding;
b) Transaction Laundering with Miscoding;
c) Third Party Transaction Laundering or Third Party Billing

When referring to illegal aggregation, the intent of the merchant is always malicious. The merchant is aware of the fact that he is obliged to report all processed and new URLs to his merchant acquirer, but purposely decided not to, because those websites might contain content in violation of rules and regulations as defined by financial institution or card schemes.

4.3.1 Transaction Laundering without Miscoding

When a legitimate and compliant merchant facilitates payments for another one of his websites which contains illegal content and/or services (unknown to the merchant acquirer), but the offered products and/or services are generally the same as those on the compliant (and reported) website, this is considered a Transaction Laundering attempt without Miscoding. The merchant is laundering the transaction through a compliant storefront.

> **Example:**
>
> The merchant Adult Limited is operating the adult website www.adultvideos.com with the MCC 5967. He is also operating the website www.forbiddencontent.com that also offers adult content but contains clear violations. The website www.forbiddencontent.com is using the payment page on www.adultvideos.com to facilitate the transactions. In this case the general business (adult business) remains the same. Although it is in attempt of Transaction Laundering, it does not involve miscoding.

The associated financial and reputational risk for the merchant acquirer can be considered very high. The merchant is operating a business that violates the rules and regulations of the card associations, therefore the acquirer can be held liable for facilitating brand damaging transactions from an unknown and unregistered source. If the card associations detect this fraudulent activity, they will impose significant fines.

4.3.2 Transaction Laundering with Miscoding

Given the fact that certain credit cards are blocked for specific MCCs[73] (e. g. for high risk businesses such as gambling or adult entertainment services), fraudulent merchants who sell illegal products or offer illegal services may launder a transaction, by using a merchant account or MID that has been set up by the acquirer for a different type of business.

---

[73] The **Merchant Category Code** (MCC or "Card Acceptor ID") is a four-digit number assigned by different credit card organizations when a merchant first starts accepting the respective form of payment. In the United States, it can be used to determine if a payment needs to be reported to the Internal Revenue Service for tax purposes. It is used to classify the activity of a merchant and allows the issuing banks to block charges from certain industries (e. g. gambling). This is used, for example, in the United States of America for the financial blocking of the card-not-present gambling industry.

Example:

A merchant operating a forex website also operates a casino website. He is processing the transactions through the same merchant account without notifying the acquirer.

In the above example, the associated financial and reputational risk for the merchant acquirer has to be considered even higher, because the merchant is operating a business that is regulated by a financial supervisory authority[74] and the associated actions might also be pursued by law enforcement. Furthermore, the additional website would require a specific operating license.[75] The acquirer is violating card association rules, because he doesn't use the appropriate MCC coding for gambling transactions.[76] Significant fines could be imposed by the card associations for this scenario.

---

[74] One of the first financial supervisory authorities that started to regulate the forex business was the CySec in Cyprus.
[75] For example, a gambling license.
[76] The responsibility of the merchant acquirer for the assignment of an appropriate MCC coding is outlined in the rules and regulations of the card associations (e. g. MasterCard Rules Section 5.7.1 (2013).

4.3.3 Third Party Transaction Laundering

Illegal Aggregation through Third Party Transaction Laundering takes place when a merchant who is neither set up as an IPSP or Payment Facilitator nor licensed to facilitate these services (e.g. e-money license), facilitates payments under his own name, on behalf of a third party (another merchant).

> **Example:**
>
> The merchant Baby Limited is facilitating transactions for their own website www.baby.com with the billing descriptor "Baby Limited / Berlin, Germany". A different merchant (the third party) is operating the website www.grownups.com This merchant utilizes the payment page on www.baby.com and informs card holders that they will be billed with the billing descriptor "Baby Limited / Berlin, Germany". This happens with the consent and approval of Baby Limited. Now Baby Limited is actively facilitating transactions on behalf of a third party (www.grownups.com) under their own name.

The associated financial and reputational risks for the merchant acquirer also have to be considered very high. The merchant is facilitating payments for a third party, a service that usually requires proper licensing provided by financial authorities. The acquirer may face heavy fines due to violation of card association rules, because the associated merchant has never been registered as an IPSP, nor as a Payment Facilitator.

Besides the above definitions, there are five types of fraud scenarios that are often misinterpreted as Transaction Laundering or as Third Party Billing attempt.

4.3.4 Affiliate Transaction Laundering

Affiliate Transaction Cleansing or Laundering is a well-known fraud scenario in the payments industry. This scenario has caused hundreds of violations, which could be traced to one fraudulent payment gateway, which offered payment services primarily in the adult industry.

In this very specific fraud scenario, the fraudulent payment gateway establishes multiple affiliate relationships with completely legitimate websites that have generous affiliate pay-outs.[77] After that, the gateway establishes commercial relationships with merchants that offer services and products which are illegal and in clear violation of rules and regulations as defined

---

[77] Affiliate networks with generous affiliate pay-outs can mostly be found in the adult entertainment industry. This is also the reason why especially this industry was in the focus of this fraudulent payment facilitator.

by the card associations. Due to the fact that these merchants have trouble gaining access to the credit card networks, they are willing to pay very high discount rates for the sole possibility of being able to accept card payments. This discount rate, charged by the fraudulent payment facilitator, ranges from 20 to over well over 70 percent.[78]

After agreeing with the relationship, the merchant implements the hosted payment page into his website. As soon as a cardholder signs up for the illegal service, the payment gateway DOES NOT put the transaction into interchange. Instead, the cardholder data is stored.[79] The cardholder receives the login credentials or the service that he has been asking for and is satisfied.

After a certain period of time, the information collected by the fraudulent payment gateway is used to sign up with one of the websites of the affiliate network they are a part of.[80] By doing so, each digital trace is obscured. For the affiliate network, the transaction looks legitimate, as even a referral URL screening[81]

---

[78] This extremely high discount rate depends on the nature of the business that the merchant is offering and also on the available affiliate programs and the associated pay-outs.
[79] The full card number, expiry date and CVV, to be precise.
[80] In some cases, the payment gateway is also injecting the harvested card details directly into the payment pages of merchants.
[81] Referral URL Screening is a technique used for the prevention of illegal aggregation.

would not discover it.[82] The fraudulent payment gateway will then collect the affiliate pay-out from their affiliate partner sites.

Although the fraudulent payment gateway does not even maintain a merchant account, it is capable of processing card payments for third parties, without being liable for violations. If an affiliate network is in place, it becomes impossible for the acquirer to detect this fraud scenario, because the transactions are generated by a legitimate website which serves as a 'mule'. From a merchant's perspective (e.g. the affiliate network) there are four different patterns that can help to identify fraudulent affiliates:

- During a manual process, the affiliate network has to look out for batch transactions and IP address concentrations of their affiliates. Fraudulent affiliates usually do not use backend postings to circumvent the electronic trail.
- The same applies to refund or cancellation requests.
- Card holders from the fraudulent affiliate almost never request chargebacks. The total number of chargeback is therefore often suspiciously low for a merchant operating a high risk business.

---

[82] The fraudulent payment gateway is only using fully compliant affiliate websites for this part of their scheme.

- The login details of the legitimate website are NEVER used, although the card holder pays for them!

4.3.5 Competitor Takedown Attack

The Competitor Takedown Attack is the advanced version of the Affiliate Transaction Cleansing scenario and has been observed for the first time in February 2013. The Competitor Takedown Attack is not aiming to facilitate illegal payments for third parties. Its main goal is to terminate the merchant account of a competitor.

To achieve their objective, the fraudster sets up dedicated websites with the purpose of collecting test transactions from the card associations. The websites are not really in use, have misleading URLs[83], have no visitors at all and are not linked to any search engine. The probability that a regular card holder would be able to identify such a website and really buy a product is extremely low (it would only be possible if the customer was actually aware of the URL). These websites look very unreliable and it is questionable if a card holder would even consider buying a product or service from such a website.

---

[83] Such a URL could be viagra1234abcdefghijklmnoprx22.com, as an example.

These websites are anonymously reported to the card associations. The fraudster only has to wait, because he knows that the transaction which hits the fraudulent website, MUST be a test transaction from a card association.

The website itself is not really functional and transactions are only stored and not processed in any way. Now that the fraudulent network is in the possession of a valid and unused test transaction of a card association, they can effectively shut down every merchant account they want to. The following example will illustrate this point:

> The card associations are investigating a case where a merchant is selling illegal pharmaceuticals (such as products requiring a prescription). The investigator responsible is facilitating the test purchase and is documenting everything with screenshots.[84]
>
> The fraudulent network receives the test transaction through one of their fake websites. Such an unused transaction is then offered for sale.[85] If a purchaser has been found, he has to

---

[84] Usually the whole procedure is documented with one ore multiple screenshots per step. The screenshots normally comprise the landing page, the checkout procedure and the payment page.
[85] During the investigation back in 2013 the price range of this attack varied between $100.000 and $500.000.

> designate a target website. This will usually be the web presence of a competitor.
>
> On the targeted website, the fraudster then buys a product that has the same or nearly the same price point as the test transaction. The checkout procedure is initiated and finally, the fraudster pays with the card details that collected before.
>
> For the card associations it looks like the targeted website facilitated the test transaction. The associated acquirer is identified and a non-compliance procedure is initiated. This potentially leads to the termination of the targeted merchant. The test transaction of the card association has been misused for fraudulent purposes. [86]

This fraud scenario is nearly impossible to detect, if you are not made aware of its existence. The merchant is not involved in the fraud – he is actually the victim – but due to the evidence provided by the card associations to the acquiring bank, he hasn't got a chance to prove his innocence. This fraud scenario is currently under heavy scrutiny. During the first phase of the investigation, over 5.000 of the described fraudulent websites have

---

[86] A flow chart that illustrates the fraud scenario can be found in the appendix of this guide.

been detected. Until today, most observed cases under investigation, were related to the sale of digital goods, digital currencies and cyber lockers.

4.3.6 Merchant Extortion / Blackmailing

During the last 18 months, the authors have been investigating several cases of affiliate Transaction Laundering attacks in connection with the described fraudulent hosted payment page. These investigations raised a lot of questions:

Until the end of 2014 it was still possible to insert transactions and therefore to identify large affiliate networks (not even high-risk affiliated) as being misused for the purpose of affiliate Transaction Laundering attacks. Since the beginning of 2015, it has been impossible to insert a transaction into the network. Although hundreds of websites have been identified, no inserted transactions have been put into interchange ever since.

> *Due to the reason that in total 14 different BINs have been used on the network and none of the transactions have been authorized or cleared, the question arises: Is the fraudulent hosted payment page operator still engaged in the affiliate Transaction Laundering business?*

Investigations revealed that the URLs of the fraudulent hosted payment page operator had none or nearly no measurable visitors. In addition, their earning on the average 'discount rate' would amount to somewhere between 20 and 25 percent on transactions of $29 to $69 (about $6 to $14).

> *As the fraudulent hosted payment page operator and the associated websites have nearly no visitors, it is questionable how profitable this system could be for them. Have they changed their business model?*

In the recent past, merchants who have not even been operating or using an affiliate network have also been attacked.[87]

> *If a website or a merchant is not utilizing any kind of affiliate system (or any kind of referral or pay-out system), how could the fraudulent hosted payment page operator use this system to draw money from it?*

It has been some time since the last attacks have been reported by merchants engaged in the adult entertainment business. Additionally, in some cases there is only ONE single attack and in

---

[87] Based on investigations conducted by Web Shield in the period of January 2015 and July 2016.

other cases investigators counted multiple ones, some even on a monthly basis.

> *As there is no real pattern behind it, why are certain merchants getting hit multiple times while the attacks at other merchants suddenly stop?*

Considering all these facts and using the abovementioned questions as a guide, leads to one simple conclusion:

The fraudulent hosted payment page operator MUST have changed their business model – otherwise it would not be profitable, especially when no referral or affiliate networks are involved.

Led by this hypothesis, multiple investigations were carried out. By this time, it had become possible to contact some of the merchants who were affected by fraudulent hosted payment page operator attacks. This revealed what happened AFTER a non-compliance action.

It became clear, that the operator (comparable with the above-described Competitor Takedown Attack!), had collected a very large number of card details that had been used in the card association's ghost shopping program.[88]

The new modus operandi involved less effort but even bigger earnings for the fraudulent operator. Like the Competitor Takedown Attack for sale, it began with the fraudulent hosted payment pager operator, collecting valid test transactions.

> **Example:**
> The fraudulent hosted payment page operator identifies a possible victim. They usually target merchants in the areas of high-risk (adult, dating and file sharing), as they know that those merchants usually do not tend to involve law enforcement for further investigations (due to the nature of their business).
> As soon as the victim is identified, the operator goes on the website, chooses a product, conducts a checkout and enters the card details, he previously collected in the same way as described in the Competitor Takedown Attack.
>
> A couple of days or weeks later, the associated merchant acquirer receives a non-compliance notification and acts according to the rules and regulations of the card association.

---

[88] The term 'ghost' or 'mystery shopping' refers to a hired shopper who anonymously visits a store to assess its products and service (online and offline).

This generally means shutting down the merchant account and/or imposing of high penalties.

As the fraudulent hosted payment page operator has been running his previous fraud scheme for a long time, it has become common knowledge to most acquirers. They therefore usually do not terminate an affected merchant account right away, but impose more extensive security procedures on the affiliate network (e.g. affiliate Due Diligence, referral URL screening), because this is still considered the most probable source of the attack.

A few days or weeks later the operator reaches out for the merchant. They only agree to communicate via Jabber (no email, no phone). When getting in touch, they offer a "service" to make these incidents stop. They ask to route all credit card transactions through their system and pay an "insurance" of $1 per transaction to them. This "insurance" covers the cessation of the attacks and provides the added service of filtering out all test transactions they are aware of.

If a merchant refuses to pay, they continue the attacks until the merchant account gets closed down or the merchant has to declare bankruptcy due to the high fines imposed by their acquirer.

Evidence has also been uncovered which reveals that these fraudsters are not after a one-time payment. Some of the attacked merchants were willing to share part of their correspondence with the extortionists with the investigators. Investigators were provided with evidence which proved that criminals declined 'bribes' they were offered, in order to stop the attacks. Evidence of the fact that these fraudsters were after processed credit card details.

The attacks by this operator resulted in the loss of huge amounts of money, terminated merchant accounts, stained records and damaged reputations. Affected merchants were faced by enormous business challenges.

It is important to understand that there is absolutely NO protection against this kind of attack. It is not a run-of-the-mill Transaction Laundering attack, but sophisticated fraud that has to be carefully investigated! Even the best anti-fraud precautions couldn't prevent such a clever, malicious attack.

Once a merchant discovers to be a victim of such attack, there are several measures that can be taken: First of all, extortion is a crime that law enforcement has to investigate, and it is absolutely necessary to press charges. All the associated evidence should be provided to the law enforcement agency (such as recordings of the conversations with the fraudster, screenshots, email conversations, affidavits, etc.). The merchant's acquirer should be provided with a proof of the charges filed and the outcome has to be shared with the card association, which has the case under investigation.

In this context it is quite obvious, that the merchant itself is not the perpetrator but the victim of this attack. In cases of a non-compliance situation, where there are doubts about the guilt of a merchant, an instant termination of the account may not be the appropriate action.

4.3.7 Transaction Collection and Testing Attacks

Research and the continuous facilitation of test transactions on websites which offer blatantly illegal or brand damaging content, reveals that there is a strong increase of websites used solely for the purpose of data or transaction collection. These sites usually offer illegal goods that have a broader potential audience, such as counterfeit goods (as shown in the example below) instead of niche products (adult content with extreme violence).

Card holders that shop and provide their card details on the payment page of such websites will be surprised to find out that no transaction is initiated. The website just collects the card holder's data for future fraudulent purposes.

Example:

The website replicabags.com is offering counterfeit bags of known brands for very low prices. Card holder 'A' conducts a checkout and enters his card details on the payment page.

After the checkout is conducted, she receives an email notification telling her the product is out of stock and no charges will appear on her credit card.

The fraudulent operator behind replicabags.com is now in the possession of the card details of card holder "A". He now tries to test, if the card is valid and can be charged. To test this, he visits the website microsoft.com to buy a software product with the valid card holder details he collected on replicabags.com.

When a card association is investigating a brand damaging website such as replicabags.com, investigators are taking screenshots along with a filing of the utilized credit card. If the fraudulent operator tests the credit card data he has collected on microsoft.com it would imply that microsoft.com facilitated the brand damaging transaction the card association has initiated, although they are only a victim of transaction testing.

Even though cases like this might look like real Transaction Laundering attempts, they differ because of the charged amount of the test transaction and the final authorization amount on the card. Another clue is the time difference and the merchant type:

the time frame between the test transaction and the first authorization often exceeds 24 hours. Furthermore, the authorization usually occurs on websites that offer digital goods or instant services.

4.3.8 Transaction Weeding Attack

Transaction weeding is a relatively new technique that has been discovered whilst conducting test transactions on brand damaging websites. Transaction weeding has been put into place by several merchants, engaged in the sale of counterfeit goods. It is based on the assumption that card associations either use randomly generated and invalid credit cards which do pass the Luhn algorithm[89], and therefore create no noticeable BIN concentration, or use valid credit cards that are not loaded and therefore automatically decline.

Transaction weeding occurs in combination with hijacked or dormant merchant accounts. Until recently, it has only been identified in conjunction with the sale of tangible goods, where

---

[89] The Luhn algorithm, also referred to as "modulus 10" or "mod 10" algorithm, is a checksum formula used to validate credit card numbers on the basis of the card number and the expiration date.

there is a delay between the purchase and the delivery of the product.

When a card holder is checking out on a website that is selling an illegal or brand damaging tangible good, the associated payment page only stores the provided credit card details if they pass the Luhn test. The website operator confirms the sale or informs the card holder that the order will soon be confirmed. The operator then uses the collected card details, either on a dormant or on a hijacked merchant account that is under his control, and initiates a very low authorization request (e.g. 1,00 €). If the card is rejected by the issuer ("Invalid Card Number", "No Card Record" or "Incorrect CVV") the website operator stops any further attempts on charging the card, as it is either a fake shopping attempt or a test transaction. Thus, the website operator protects his real merchant account which he uses to run the full charge if the card was successfully authorized.

These activities by fraudulent actors are evidence of the fact that the use of fake or randomly generated credit cards for ghost shopping is problematic. They only identify the security layer account the fraudster has set up between the website and his real merchant account. In a recent case, the merchant account of a very reputable brand was hijacked by a counterfeit merchant and all initial authorizations were made, using the name and merchant account of this well-known brand.

Transaction Laundering attacks need to be investigated into great detail, in order to discover if the merchant was the perpetrator or the victim of one of the above described fraud attacks, or to find out if criminals have found an even more devious way to exploit their victims.

4.4 Aggregation Detection

Fully understanding the different varieties of Aggregation, Transaction Laundering and associated fraud attacks, helps to set up appropriate detection and monitoring tools to minimize risks and prevent Transaction Laundering attacks. As an example, we will explain four anti-Transaction Laundering tools and services, offered by Web Shield[90] in detail.

4.4.1 PULSE Transaction Laundering

Incompliant Aggregation as outlined in section 4.2 can be identified with the "PULSE Transaction Laundering" tool. On the basis of the processed URL list of the merchant acquirer, the

---

[90] Additional information is available online (**www.webshield.com**).

system identifies other websites that belong to the same merchant; websites which are most probably facilitating transactions through the same acquirer. Those identified websites DO NOT contain an illegal service or product and therefore do only represent a small risk. When it comes to high-risk business, the assessment changes, as high-risk business usually requires a registration. It is therefore essential to be aware of all processed URLs of a merchant.

PULSE Transaction Laundering provides the acquirer with an updated list of URLs on a monthly basis.

4.4.2 Transaction Laundering Incident Alert

Illegal Aggregation through Transaction Laundering (with and without miscoding) as well as Third Party Billing can be detected with the Transaction Laundering Incident Alert. It identifies websites that are clearly promoting or selling illegal products and services and are unknown to the merchant acquirer. Based on the provided processed URL list, the system identifies connected websites that are offering illegal services and/or products.

In a second step, all websites are scraped and analyzed to verify if they allow their customers to pay online. For every reported case, a checkout procedure and test transaction (real card) is initiated to identify the associated merchant account and the acquirer. The process is properly documented with screenshots. During the last step, a report is generated that highlights what illegal products and/or services are being offered.

4.4.3 Referral URL Screening

If the acquirer is providing a hosted payment page to merchants, he can also include a Referral URL Screening which requires the integration of a script on the hosted payment page. The system operates with a whitelist and a blacklist to differentiate between familiar and unknown websites. The Referral URL Screening instantly reviews the referral URL for hard content violations (BRAM/GBPP) and recommends whether to accept or to decline the transaction.

4.4.4 Transaction Laundering Investigations

In case of one of the above mentioned fraud attempts (Affiliate Transaction Cleansing, Competitor Takedown Attacks and Merchant Extortion), Web Shield offers investigation services to identify whether a Transaction Laundering attempt or a Fraud Attack by a Third Party has occurred. This service includes a full review of all associated merchant documents, screening of the associated websites and a written analysis of the investigation.

5. Conclusion

The Global e-Commerce boom has resulted in profitable business for all stakeholders involved. Unfortunately, fraudsters profit in the shadow of growing e-Commerce, by inventing sophisticated, increasingly complex and malicious Fraud scenarios with great impact on their victims. The recent case around German dating operator Lovoo[91], accused of using fake profiles and chat robots to deceive card holders, illustrates the complex task of Underwriters who need to identify, investigate, validate and assess Risk at a daily base in order to come to a balanced decision. It is crucial to stay up to date about new scenarios and to understand recent fraud attacks, in order to prevent reputational damage and financial losses. Understanding the various types of risk indicators and recognizing the devastating impact when these risk indicators are overlooked or ignored, helps Underwriters come to a balanced risk assessment at the end of the Due Diligence process. This second edition aims to provide Underwriters and Risk Managers with an Investigation Strategy, as developed by industry professionals with years of solid experience in this business. A checklists or scoring matrix, easily adapted to the specific risk appetite of the acquirer, can form the base for an auditable framework. Even though this step-by-step approach is time consuming, each step in this investigative risk

---

[91] http://www.heise.de/newsticker/meldung/Dating-Dienst-Lovoo-Fast-1-2-Millionen-Euro-Schaden-durch-Betrug-3235838.html (26.08.2016).

analysis is crucial in order to reach to a sensible conclusion, whether to accept or decline a merchant at the end of the KYC procedures.

Identifying concrete risk indicators during an investigation converts the 'gut feeling' of experienced Underwriters auditable. The final Investigation Summary is a Report which should include all associated findings. This isn't only a practical case management document, but it also serves as proof of evidence, if the acquirer runs into unexpected legal issues.

As described in the previous edition, the introduced tools and procedures as described throughout both best practice guides should be considered as part of a constantly evolving process and not as a rigid series of individual check procedures.

As an illustration of this paradigm, this book has added important research resources to the previously discussed ones. Applying these during an investigation, improves the chance of identifying additional websites, controlled and/or operated by an investigated merchant or by a third party. The described tools enable Underwriters to identify indicators for possible aggregation attempts, before the merchant has even been boarded.

This second edition explores Aggregation (Transaction Laundering) and its various forms into great detail. The additional fraud scenarios described in this guide, help Underwriters to assess non-compliance situations with a credit card association. As fraud scenarios are constantly changing and fraudsters adapt their schemes to avoid detection by the merchant acquirer, it has to be understood that there is no easy protection against fraud attacks, no matter how sophisticated the implemented detection and monitoring tools are.

Notwithstanding this harsh reality, the aim of this Guide is the same of that of the previous Guide: The protection against avoidable financial loss and reputational damage of all parties involved in the complex and expanding e-payments ecosystem.

Glossary

Glossary

Acquirer - The "acquirer", "merchant acquirer", "acquiring bank" or "merchant bank" enters into an agreement (merchant agreement), authorizing merchants to accept the association's credit cards, submit their merchants' transactions into the association's interchange system for payment from issuing banks, and maintain accounts and related records on their merchant clients (Office, 2010).

Acquirer hopping - During Acquirer hopping, the merchant sets up an acceptance contract with a credit card acquirer, then performs a fraudulent act and afterwards turns to another acquirer (usually in another country or continent) in order to repeat this.

Billing Descriptor - The billing descriptor (or merchant descriptor) is the way a merchant's name appears on a credit card statement and is set up together with the merchant identification number when the merchant account is setup. It is used by the credit card holder, to identify the merchant that initiated the charge. Credit card organizations use the billing descriptor within their monitoring systems (e. g. chargeback or fraud monitoring).

Burn MID – A Burn MID refers to a very specific merchant setup where the merchant is facilitating an extremely high number of unauthorized charges on stolen credit cards with very low ticket sizes, in general below 50,00 USD. A Burn MID can usually only be used once and if so, not for more than 24 hours. In most cases it requires also the active involvement of an employee of the merchant acquirer to circumvent the general velocity checks in the banking system.

Declaration of Trust - is an assertion by a property owner that he or she holds the property or estate for the benefit of another person.

Card-Not-Present - A card not present transaction, also known as CNP, MO/TO, Mail Order / Telephone Order represents a payment card transaction, where the cardholder does not or cannot physically present the card to the merchant, at the time when the payment is initiated.

Copycat Website - A copycat website is a website designed to give the consumer the impression that he has accessed a site known to him. This way the login or payment data of customers can be intercepted and then used fraudulently by the operator of the copycat website.

Chargeback - In this Guide, book a Chargeback is a return of funds to a consumer/card holder, initiated by the issuing bank of the payment method used by a consumer to settle a debt.

Ghost shopping - The term ghost shopping refers to a hired shopper who contacts a store anonymously, in order to assess its products and service (online and offline).

Issuer - The "issuer", "issuing bank" or "card issuer" extends credits to cardholders, establish the terms of cardholders' accounts (e. g. credit limits), collect debts, and maintain accounts and cardholder records (Office, 2010).

Load Balancing - Load balancing in the card payments-context refers to a performance optimization tactic that provides fault-tolerance by splitting incoming transactions across several MIDs, in order to circumvent certain monitoring procedures of the merchant acquirer or the card associations.

Merchant Category Code - The Merchant Category Code (MCC or "Card Acceptor ID") is a four-digit number, assigned by different credit card organizations when a merchant first starts accepting the respective form of payment. In the United

States, it can be used, to determine if a payment needs to be reported to the Internal Revenue Service for tax purposes. It is used to classify the activity of a merchant and allows the issuing banks to block charges from certain industries (e. g. gambling). In the USA, it is used to block the CNP gambling industry.

Merchant Identification Number – The Merchant Identification Number (MID) is a unique identification number assigned by the payment institution (such as an acquiring bank) to a merchant account.

Mystery Shopping – see „Ghost Shopping".

Politically exposed persons - Politically exposed persons are understood to be persons entrusted with prominent public functions, their immediate family members or persons known to be close associates of such persons.

Power of Attorney - or letter of attorney is written document in which one person (in general the director) appoints another person to act as an agent on his behalf, thus conferring authority on the agent to perform certain acts or functions on behalf of the director. Powers of attorney are routinely granted to allow the agent to take care of a variety of transactions for the principal, such as executing a stock power, handling a tax audit, or maintaining a safe-deposit box.

RMA - A return merchandise authorization (RMA) is sometimes a part of the procedure of returning a product in order to receive a refund or replacement. The cardholder must contact the merchant or the fulfillment center to obtain an authorization to return the product. The RMA number must then be included in the returned product's packaging. In general merchants that use RMAs do not accept any returns without this number. This technique is often seen in the areas of the sale of nutraceuticals, mostly to increase the barrier on returning the product and avoiding the necessity of refunds. In many cases it although has a different impact and increases the number of chargebacks as cardholders then prefer to go the easier way.

Sponsored Merchant - A sponsored merchant is a merchant, whose payment services are provided by a Payment Facilitator or Internet Payment Service Provider and NOT directly by the acquirer.

Underwriting – In this Best Practice Guide, underwriting is considered to be the business and credit analysis, which precedes the acceptance of a specific payment method (e. g. a credit card merchant account), based on information provided by the merchant and gathered by the Underwriter throughout the Due Diligence procedure.

About the Authors

Christian André Chmiel

Christian A. Chmiel, CEO of Web Shield Limited in London, is responsible for the development and implementation of new investigation techniques and research tools to identify fraudulent or brand damaging online merchants. Before, Christian has served as the Deputy Head of Compliance with a German merchant acquirer, where he specialized in online fraud investigations, credit card compliance and underwriting for acquiring banks.

Christian has studied in Hamburg (Germany), Lincoln (UK) and Gloucestershire (UK). He holds a bachelor's and diploma degree in European Business Administration, is a Certified Fraud Examiner (ACFE) and a Certified High-Risk Underwriter (WSA). He is author and co-author of several books in the fields of fraud, investigations and accounting.

Markus Prause

Markus Prause, VP Underwriting and Monitoring of Web Shield Limited in London, is responsible for the areas of online investigation, merchant monitoring and client integrity. Before, Markus worked for a German financial institution and two merchant acquirers in the field of risk and compliance. He is specialized in the area of on-boarding investigations and non-compliance investigations, client integrity retention and risk consulting. Markus is a Certified High-Risk Underwriter (WSA) and an instructor of the Web Shield Academy.

About the Editors

Shanty Elena van de Sande

Shanty Elena van de Sande is a freelance B2B Content Writer with almost 20 years of experience in corporate and innovative ICT companies. She worked 10 years for HP, after which she joined the Product Management Team of Risk Management solutions provider Syfact (now NICE Actimize). As Payvision's Research Analyst-B2B Content Writer, Shanty wrote a series of Industry White Papers, which explore trends and business opportunities in the growing (mobile) e-commerce and CNP card payments industry. For more information, please visit: **www.elenavandesande.com**

Johannes Rosenau

Johannes Rosenau heads Web Shield's Marketing Department and as such is responsible for internal communications and knowledge management as well as advertisements and public relations. He graduated from the Martin-Luther-University Halle-Wittenberg with a Master's degree in Media and Communications studies.

References

Albrechtslund. (2016, 08 25). Online social networking as participatory surveillance. Retrieved from First Monday - Peer Reviewed Journal on the Internet: http://journals.uic.edu/ojs/index.php/fm/article/view/2142/1949#author

Chmiel, C., (2010). Online-Investigation im Due Diligence-Prozess von Acquirer-Banken, BOD.

Chmiel, C.& Prause, M. (2015). Fundamentals of Card-not-Present Merchant Acceptance: Best Practice Guide for Underwriters – Edition 2016. Leipzig. Web Shield Services.

Goldman, Barbara; Borchewski, Michail (2008): Traced! Online-Personenrecherche: So googeln Sie Schuldner, Nachbarn, Bewerber oder Ihr nächstes Date, BoD Verlag

Grabe, O. (2006). Die Risikozuordnung im US-amerikanischen Kreditkartenverfahren: Mit besonderer Berücksichtigung des Kreditkartenmissbrauchs im E-Commerce. Göttingen: Vandenhoeck & Ruprecht.

Haythornthwaite, C. (2005). Social networks and Internet connectivity effects. Information, Communication, & Society.

MasterCard. (2007). MasterCard Dictionary. O'Fallon: MasterCard Worldwide.

MasterCard (2009): MATCH User Manual, MasterCard Worldwide

MasterCard (2008): Quick Reference Booklet, MasterCard Worldwide

MasterCard. (2013). MasterCard Rules. Purchase: MasterCard Worldwide.

Visa Europe. (2009). Acquirer Risk Management Best Practices Guide. London: Visa Europe Services Inc.

Visa (2007): Rules for Visa Merchants - Card Acceptance and Chargeback Management Guidelines, Visa USA Inc.

Visa Inc. (2004). Card Acceptance and Chargeback Management Guide for Visa Merchants. Foster City: Visa.

Visa Inc. (2009). Global Airline Acquiring Best Practice Guide. New York: Visa Inc.

Visa Europe. (2015). Operating Regulations. London: Visa Europe Services Inc.

Worthington, S. (1995). The cashless society. International Journal of Retail & Distribution Management, pp. 31-40.

Recommended Books

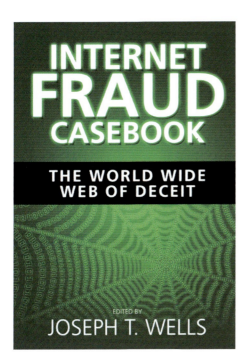

Internet Fraud Casebook (English)

Web scams targeting the unemployed. Computer fraud. Online auction fraud. Market manipulation schemes. While the Internet offers a global marketplace for consumers and businesses, it also presents endless potential for crooks and scammers.

The same scams found through the mail and phone have crept their way onto the Internet and into e-mail, with new variations of cyber scams emerging all the time.

Internet Fraud Casebook: The World Wide Web of Deceit presents the collected insights of some of the most experienced fraud examiners around the world.

Handpicked and edited by Joseph Wells, the founder and Chairman of the Association of Certified Fraud Examiners (ACFE) — the world's leading anti-fraud organization — this collection of revealing case studies sheds new light into the dark corners of online fraud. Some of the forty-one cases in Internet Fraud Casebook include:

- "**Behind the** Mask," Christian A. Chmiel
- "**Dangerous Diet**," Nancy E. Jones
- "**A Business within a Business**," Alan Greggo

Each case in this indispensable casebook explores various kinds of Internet fraud as well as their assorted sub-schemes: phishing, online auction fraud, security breaches, counterfeiting, and others. In addition, each case offers an informative and entertaining look into the complex social factors behind fraudulent behavior on the Web. The observations of each fraud examiner, drawn from years of practical experience, provide readers with invaluable perspectives, many of which have never before been conveyed publicly.

Forming a comprehensive picture of the many types of Internet fraud and how they are analyzed across industries and throughout the world, Internet Fraud Casebook equips you with authoritative, proven investigative and preventive guidance.

Publisher: John Wiley & Sons; (20. August 2010)
Language: Englisch
ISBN-10: 0470643633
ISBN-13: 978-0470643631

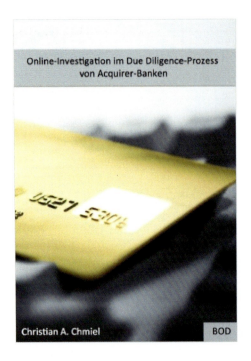

**Online Investigation im Due Diligence-Prozess
von Acquirer-Banken** (German)

In den letzten Jahren hat sich die Art des Kreditkartenbetrugs weltweit schrittweise verändert. Der Kreditkartenmissbrauch durch den Online-Händler wurde eine immer größere Bedrohung sowohl für die Kreditkartenorganisationen an sich als auch für die angeschlossenen Acquirer-Banken. Das vorliegende Buch ist eine Best-Practice-Lösung für Mitarbeiter von

Acquirer-Banken, die im Bereich Betrugs-, Compliance- oder Risikomanagement tätig sind. Es wird auf verschiedene Vorgehensweisen zur Online-Investigation, die dazu notwendigen Werkzeuge sowie die Interpretationsmöglichkeiten eingegangen, um potentielle Betrugsabsichten von Online-Händlern schon vor der dem Anschluss an das Kreditkartennetzwerk identifizieren zu können.

Publisher: BOD; (25. August 2010)
Language: German
ISBN-10: 3839189039
ISBN-13: 978-3839189030

Fundamentals of Card-not-Present Merchant Acceptance: A Best Practice Guide for Underwriters – Edition 2016 (English)

As international e-Commerce thrives and e-Payment volume rises, so does cybercrime. Credit cards are still #1 CNP payment method worldwide and form an attractive target for fraudsters, involved in financial crime. Financial Institutions are forced to adapt their Due Diligence procedures, in order to be legally compliant and to mitigate risk. Criminals have shifted their "modus operandus" and are increasingly using web shops to commit large-scale fraud. Card fraud, committed by malicious online merchants, has become a growing threat to Acquiring Banks and payment service providers (PSP) and has led to reputational damage, financial losses and fines from the card organizations. The Authors of this Best Practice Guide are Industry Professionals, with extensive experience in the online Payment Industry, resulting in a practical manual for professionals in Risk Management departments of e-Payments facilitators. The various chapters in this Guide, explain the different Fraud Scenarios and zoom in on recent Fraud cases. The various analytical tools and investigative methodology available to detect, analyse and prevent fraud before merchant acceptance are highlighted. Fundamentals of Due Diligence processes and KYC screening procedures are outlined, including all crucial steps during the EDD on-boarding phase. Underwriters and Risk Managers in the Payment Acquiring business will find this book very useful, as it provides added value and expertise necessary to protect financial institution against financial loss, avoidable chargebacks and reputational damage; expertise which is crucial for all stakeholders involved in profitable cross-border e-commerce.

Publisher: Web Shield Services; (1. January 2016)
Language: English
ISBN-10: 3000509372
ISBN-13: 978-3000509377

Recommended Courses

Certified High Risk Underwriter (WSA)

Be prepared for a new criminal threat

Growing pressure from regulators, the fourth EU Anti-Money Laundering directive, intense press coverage of scandals and the constant evolution of the legal framework have brought this topic to the top of Management's agenda.

Companies oftentimes masquerade as legitimate businesses for the purpose of laundering their money. What you see when you interact with such a company is just the peak of the iceberg – a small, but legitimate seeming part of a greater operation. Although the majority of their activities is concealed from plain sight, they still pose a threat to you. Learn to expose these hidden depths with our "Certified High-Risk Underwriter" course.

What you will take home

The course will give you the specialized knowledge for implementing meaningful due diligence measures over a broad range of different industries. How do you verify documents yourself, identify the beneficial owner and untangle complex organizational structures? Above and beyond these fundamentals, our lecturers will open the digital forensics tool-kit for you. In the many hands-on case studies, you will learn to conduct effective open-source intelligence gathering and come to your own conclusions about who you are dealing with: perfectly legitimate business or sophisticated fraudster?

At the conclusion of the course, you will have the chance to put your knowledge to the test and earn your certificate.

Find out more about upcoming events or request your own in-house course! Just contact **academy@webshieldltd.com**

Web Shield Academy
Nordstrasse 1
04105 Leipzig, Germany
www.webshield.com
academy@webshieldltd.com

Appendix A - Transaction Laundering

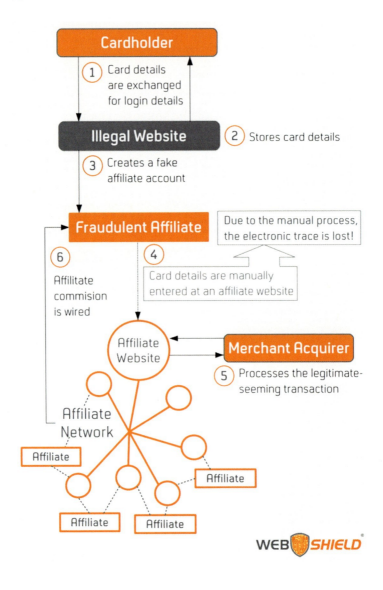

Appendix B - Flow Chart of the Competitor Takedown Attack

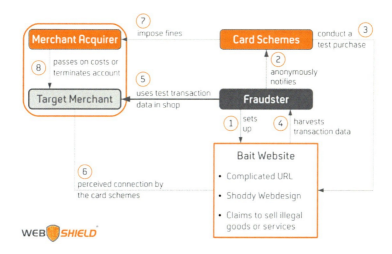